YORK NOTES

Romeo and Juliet

William Shakespeare

Notes by N. H. Keeble

 Longman   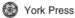 York Press

The right of N. H. Keeble to be identified as Author of this Work has been asserted by him in accordance with the Copyright, Designs and Patents Act 1988

YORK PRESS
322 Old Brompton Road, London SW5 9JH

Pearson Education Limited
Edinburgh Gate, Harlow,
Essex CM20 2JE, United Kingdom
Associated companies, branches and representatives throughout the world

First published 1998
Third impression 1999

ISBN 0-582-32906-X

Designed by Vicki Pacey, Trojan Horse, London
Phototypeset by Gem Graphics, Trenance, Mawgan Porth, Cornwall
Produced by Addison Wesley Longman China Limited, Hong Kong

CONTENTS

PART ONE

INTRODUCTION

HOW TO STUDY A PLAY

Studying on your own requires self-discipline and a carefully thought-out work plan in order to be effective.

- Drama is a special kind of writing (the technical term is 'genre') because it needs a performance in the theatre to arrive at a full interpretation of its meaning. Try to imagine that you are a member of the audience when reading the play. Think about how it could be presented on the stage, not just about the words on the page.

- Drama is always about conflict of some sort (which may be below the surface). Identify the conflicts in the play and you will be close to identifying the large ideas or themes which bind all the parts together.

- Make careful notes on themes, character, plot and any sub-plots of the play.

- Why do you like or dislike the characters in the play? How do your feelings towards them develop and change?

- Playwrights find non-realistic ways of allowing an audience to see into the minds and motives of their characters, for example soliloquy, aside or music. Consider how such dramatic devices are used in the play you are studying.

- Think of the playwright writing the play. Why were these particular arrangements of events, characters and speeches chosen?

- Cite exact sources for all quotations, whether from the text itself or from critical commentaries. Wherever possible find your own examples from the play to back up your opinions.

- Always express your ideas in your own words.

This York Note offers an introduction to *Romeo and Juliet* and cannot substitute for close reading of the text and the study of secondary sources.

Romeo and Juliet is amongst the most famous of Shakespeare's plays. Since its first performance at the end of the sixteenth century it has been a constant presence in our culture, referred to in countless books. It has been reworked in opera, ballet, film, music and fiction. Through his depiction of their fate Shakespeare created one of the icons of our culture and raised Romeo and Juliet to rank beside Lancelot and Guinevere, Tristan and Iseult, as doomed lovers caught up in one of the three great tragic love stories of the Western world. Many who have never even read a word of Shakespeare will recognise their names, and there can hardly be an educated person in the English-speaking world who has not heard of the feud between Montagues and Capulets and of this ill-fated love story.

The self-destructive passion of lovers at odds with the expectations and obligations of the world in which they live is at the heart of two of Shakespeare's tragedies. *Romeo and Juliet* is distinguished from the other (*Antony and Cleopatra*) as a tragedy of *young* love. Its extraordinary power has much to do with the way it recreates the passionate extremism of youth, the excess of its hopes and its despairs, the clash between its idealism and the bitterness of experienced adults. It captures both, on the one hand, the innocence of youth, confident it can overcome (or ignore) the world and, on the other, its passionate self-centredness, its determination to count no cost in seeking the satisfaction of its desire. As the poet John Donne succinctly put it in a poem probably written at the same time as this play, the world of their love is so self-sufficient that for Romeo and Juliet, wholly absorbed in each other, 'Nothing else is' ('The Sun Rising'). That is both the splendour and the tragedy of their story.

And yet, for all the power of its depiction of adolescent passion in conflict with a world riven by partisan hatred, materialism and hypocrisy, it is not easy for a modern reader to get on terms with this play. It fails to meet many of the expectations which we bring to a text and many of its features can appear strange, even slightly silly. For this there are three reasons: first, the nature of the stage for which Shakespeare wrote; secondly, the conventions and style of Elizabethan literature; thirdly, the passage of time and changes in the English language since the play's composition. Because of these features the text presents modern readers with many questions which make it difficult to respond positively to the play. Why, for example, is the action so improbable, so unrealistic? Why is the language so ornate? How are we to believe in these characters? If they are supposed to be Italians, why do they sound so English?

It is the purpose of this Note to answer some of these questions and to discuss some of these difficulties, and so to clear the way to an appreciation of the play and an understanding of why it should hold such a central place in our literary history. We shall consider not only questions of form and style but also the larger issues raised by the text: discussion of why Romeo and Juliet die, for example, leads to reflection on the nature of tragedy. Their fate raises questions about the duty of children, of parents, of families, of the Church and of the State. The suddenness of their love, others' views of it and the difficulties it encounters prompt questions about the nature of love and of sexual desire. Examination of these and other aspects of the play is intended to help the reader to experience the affective power of Shakespeare's poetry and the deeply moving, but also deeply perplexing, tragic world of his play.

PART TWO

SUMMARIES

Romeo and Juliet was published in a **quarto** in 1597 and again in 1599 (these two editions are distinguished as Q1 and Q2). Q1 is a bad quarto: it prints the text of the play as two or three of the actors who took part in a performance remembered it. Such a memorised version is obviously unreliable. But although Q1 is short and often confused, it does reflect an actual performance of Shakespeare's time. It has unusually full stage directions and must often record what the actors actually said and did on the stage. (Q1 is printed as an appendix in H.H. Furness, ed., *Romeo and Juliet*, New Variorum Edition of Shakespeare, NY, 1963.)

Q2, on the other hand, is based upon a written copy of the play, but although it is fuller and more reliable than Q1, it still has many errors. For example, the four lines II.2.188–91 are printed not only there but again at the beginning of the Friar's speech which opens II.3. A modern editor has to decide where he or she thinks Shakespeare meant them to be. Nor does Q2 always make clear who is speaking: the parts of the musicians at the end of IV.5, for example, are not clearly distinguished.

It may even have been Shakespeare's own manuscript that the printer of Q2 worked with, for quite often it prints what appears to be a rough draft of lines, followed by a second version. For example, I.2.14 and 15 look like two versions of the same line. Or again, in Romeo's long speech to the Friar in III.3, lines 40–4 repeat themselves, using almost the same words. Almost certainly, Shakespeare did not intend this repetition, and it looks as though the printer did not notice that one of the lines had been crossed out.

One passage of a play does exist in Shakespeare's handwriting. This is his contribution of nearly 150 lines to *Sir Thomas More*, a play by other dramatists. This passage is printed in the editions of Shakespeare's *Complete Works*, edited by Peter Alexander, London, 1951, and by Stanley Wells and Gary Taylor, Oxford, 1988. A glance at it will show the kind of difficulties the printer of Q2 probably dealt with: spelling, corrections, line and speech divisions all present problems in this manuscript as Shakespeare left it.

A third edition (Q3, 1609) was based on Q2, and so were a fourth (Q4, 1622) and a fifth (Q5, 1637). These texts contain some corrections of errors in Q2, but we cannot know if they were simply the printer's guesses or were actually what Shakespeare wrote. Besides, they carried on many of the old errors, and added new ones of their own. The Folio text of 1623 was based on Q3. Modern editors therefore work with Q1 and Q2 as the earliest versions on which all the others are based. They will make Q2 their main text (as the fuller version), and check it against Q1 when they suspect an error. They will also see if later versions offer a possible correction in such cases.

As an example of the difficulties, take the variation in only one word in the printed texts. Romeo addresses Juliet in II.2.167. What he says appears like this in the different editions:

Madame? (Q1)
My Neece? (Q2, Q3, F1)
My Deere? (Q4, Q5)
My Sweet? (F2, F3, F4)

In the New Penguin edition, 'neece' is preferred and spelled 'nyas', but other modern editors print 'sweet'. When there are so many choices over a single word, it is clear that modern editions of the complete texts will vary considerably from each other.

These notes take as their text the New Penguin Shakespeare edition of the play, edited by T. J. B. Spencer, Penguin, 1967, and frequently reprinted thereafter. This has an excellent introduction, and very full and helpful notes in the commentary which follows the text. There is also a discussion of the textual problems of the play. Other available paperback editions are given in Further Reading.

SYNOPSIS

In Act I Romeo, infatuated by Rosaline (whom we never meet), goes to the party given by Lord Capulet on Sunday evening in order to see her. There he meets Juliet and, forgetting Rosaline, falls in love with her (I.5). However, the Act ends with the lovers discovering each other's identity, and hence the threatening fact that, as Juliet is a Capulet and Romeo a

Montague, they belong to feuding families who would never let them see each other. In Act II the course of their love nevertheless moves quickly. That night, in the famous balcony scene (II.2), they exchange vows, and the following afternoon they are married secretly by Friar Laurence (II.6).

In Act III the tragic counter-movement begins. Romeo had not been invited to Lord Capulet's party, and the Capulet Tybalt is determined not to let his intrusion pass unpunished. In the quarrel and fight that follows in the first scene of Act III Romeo's friend Mercutio is killed by Tybalt and Romeo avenges his friend's death by killing Tybalt. For this, Romeo is banished from Verona by the Prince, Escalus. The Friar advises Romeo to leave Verona to live in the nearby city of Mantua until there is an opportunity to proclaim his marriage to Juliet publicly (III.2), and so, after spending Monday night with Juliet, Romeo leaves (III.5). Juliet's parents mistake her sorrow at Romeo's leaving for grief for her dead cousin, Tybalt, and think to overcome it by insisting that on the next Thursday she should marry her suitor, Count Paris (III.4). This Juliet refuses to do, and her father threatens never to see her again if she persists in this disobedience (III.5).

At the beginning of Act IV Juliet seeks the advice of Friar Laurence. He suggests that the night before her marriage she should take a potion which will make her appear dead on her wedding morning. She would then be placed in the family vault, from which he and Romeo could rescue her when she awakens, and Romeo could take her back to live with him in Mantua. To this she agrees, and so submits to her father who, overjoyed at this change of heart, brings the wedding forward to the next day, Wednesday (IV.2). The Friar meanwhile writes to Romeo to tell him of the scheme and bids him return from Mantua. However, while all else goes according to plan, this letter is never delivered (V.2). Instead, Romeo is told by his servant that Juliet is really dead (V.1). On hearing the news, Romeo returns to the Capulet vault, where Juliet lies, there to poison himself. When Juliet wakes up in the vault, and sees Romeo's body, she stabs herself in her grief. The deaths of both their heirs, explained by Friar Laurence in a summary of the plot (V.3.229–69), reconcile the Capulet and Montague families.

PROLOGUE   The Chorus introduces the matter of the play in a sonnet
addressed to the audience

The first four lines (or **quatrain**) prepare the audience to see the long-standing hostility between two equally noble Veronese families (the Capulets and Montagues) breaking out anew; the second quatrain foretells the healing of this feud through the deaths of a pair of ill-fated lovers, children of these families (Romeo and Juliet). This is to be the matter of the play, which will last two hours. The Chorus's concluding two lines (or **couplet**) asks the audience to watch with patience while the actors do their best to please them.

> The Chorus's introduction stresses the tragic nature of the play – we are not prepared by him for the comic figure of the Nurse or the wit of Mercutio. Although the word *chorus* is taken from Classical drama, where the Chorus consists of a group of characters commenting upon the action, the Chorus here (as in such other Shakespeare plays as *Henry V*, *Henry VIII* and *Troilus and Cressida)* is a single figure.

dignity noble rank
mutiny violent quarrelling
civil belonging to citizens and civilised
star-crossed thwarted by the influence of the stars, ill-fated
misadventured tragic
traffic business
miss be wanting, seem to be inadequate in our performance

ACT I

SCENE 1   The feud between Montagues and Capulets, and Romeo's
love for Rosaline, are introduced

Time: 9 a.m. Sunday morning (I.1.160–1) (How the day is discovered is explained in Time in the Play)
Benvolio, a Montague, tries to stop a quarrel between Capulet and Montague servants, but is taunted to fight in earnest with Tybalt, a Capulet. The uproar caused by Veronese citizens joining in the fray brings Lord and Lady Capulet and Lord and Lady Montague to the scene and,

finally, the Prince of Verona, Escalus, who commands peace and decrees that any further fighting between the two families will be punished by death. When the stage is cleared, Benvolio explains to Montague how the fight began. We then learn of Romeo's strangely solitary habits and depressed mood, which his father, Montague, is unable to understand. As Romeo enters, Benvolio resolves to discover what troubles him. Romeo admits he is sad because the lady he loves does not return his affection. Should he, as Benvolio advises, try to forget her by seeking out other women, their appearance would only emphasise how much the beauty of the woman he loves excels theirs.

The play begins like a comedy, with the boastful and bawdy exchanges of the Capulet servants Sampson and Gregory who, meeting Abram and another Montague servant, embark on a quarrel with them which their evident lack of heroism renders comic. Through the comedy of the servants aping their social betters, the play mocks the seriousness with which Montagues and Capulets take their feud and alerts the audience to the absurdity of their obsession. In their case, however, it will prove tragic.

carry coals a dirty task performed by the lowest servants; proverbially, to put up with being humiliated

colliers coal merchants; colloquial term of abuse

choler anger; pun on 'collier'

draw draw our swords

collar hangman's noose; pun on 'collier' and 'choler'

moved aroused, angered

To move ... art moved Gregory now uses 'move' literally, and so means that in a quarrel Sampson would run, not hold his ground and fight

dog worthless fellow

take the wall walk along the side of the path next to a building (and thus avoid the mess in the gutters and rubbish thrown from windows above); Sampson is boasting that he would not step aside for any Montague

For the weakest ... wall Gregory turns Sampson's boast against him by using a proverb which again uses 'wall' but means that the less powerful are pushed aside by the stronger

weaker vessels Elizabethan thinking generally assumed that woman was inferior to man and used this Biblical phrase (I Peter 3:7) to express the idea

thrust Sampson applies Gregory's words to women, who are pushed against the wall by their lovers

civil Sampson is being **ironic**

maidenhead virginity

sense meaning

sense feeling

stand have an erection

fish (slang) women

poor-John hake, a kind of fish, dried and salted, eaten by poor people

Fear me not do not be afraid for me, on my account; in the next line Gregory takes the words in the sense 'do not be afraid of me'

marry (mild exclamation) By the Virgin Mary

list please

I will bite ... thumb insulting gesture such as might provoke a quarrel

Here comes one ... kinsmen Gregory, a Capulet servant, must mean Tybalt, though a Montague, Benvolio, enters first

washing slashing

What, art thou drawn have you your sword out

heartless hinds a pun on female deer ('hinds') without their stags ('harts'), meaning cowardly ('heartless') women servants ('hinds')

bills, and partisans kinds of pikes

Hold me not Montague speaks to his wife, as is clear from the next line

Profaners misusers

neighbour-stainèd stained with the blood of neighbours

mistempered wrongly made ('tempered') because you use them in bad temper

airy vague; this is all we hear of the cause of the quarrel between Capulets and Montagues

Cankered with peace grown rusty through lack of use

cankered hate malignant hate

pay ... peace pay the penalty for breaking the peace

new abroach newly open

on part and part on one side or the other

drive drove

most sought ... be found wanted above all to be where fewest people might be found

humour inclination

Aurora goddess of dawn

heavy sad

pens shuts

portentous ominous

humour mood

by any means in every way possible

close reserved

sounding fathoming, being understood (literally, 'measured')

envious malicious

shrift confession

But new only just

makes would make

view appearance; Benvolio thinks of Cupid, god of love

muffled Cupid was often depicted with eyes covered, to signify that love is blind

still always

create created; Romeo, trying in vain to describe his feelings, in frustration calls on 'anything', the first thing that God created from nothing, for example

coz cousin

propagate increase

discreet discriminating

A choking ... sweet a poison which chokes (the life out of you) and a preserved sweet (which is delicious and desirable)

Soft go softly, that is, wait a moment

sadness earnest

groan Romeo takes 'sadness' in the sense of 'sorrow'

sadly seriously

aimed so near guessed as much

fair easily seen; a play on 'fair', meaning beautiful, in the preceding line

Cupid's arrow anyone pierced by an arrow Cupid's bow would fall in love

Dian's wit the cleverness and skill of Diana, goddess of chastity, who will preserve herself from Romeo's amorous advances

stay submit to, endure

ope open

lap (euphemism) Romeo wishes her to open her legs for sexual intercourse

store wealth

sparing in that ... waste because, abstaining from sex, she will deprive the future of her offspring

starved killed

beauties beautiful women

in question to mind

masks ladies of rank would wear masks at public festivities

passing surpassing, exceptionally

note reminder

pay pay you for that, that is, Benvolio will teach Romeo to forget

die in debt die with payment unmade, die in the attempt

SCENE 2 **Romeo and Benvolio decide to attend the Capulet party in order to see Rosaline**

Time: Sunday afternoon (I.1.100; 2.1–2)

Count Paris appears for the first time and asks Capulet for permission to marry his daughter (Juliet). Capulet hesitates, because Juliet is so young, but says he would agree if Juliet consents. Inviting Paris to the feast that is to be held that night, Capulet advises him to look at the ladies there to be sure it is Juliet whom he would like to marry. As the servant whom Capulet directs to invite his guests cannot read their names on the list he is given, he asks Romeo, who has entered with Benvolio, to read them for him. Rosaline, the lady Romeo loves, is one of the guests: because of this, Romeo and Benvolio decide to go to the feast, although they have not been invited. Benvolio hopes to show Romeo that Rosaline cannot equal the beauty of the other ladies present; Romeo wants simply to see Rosaline.

The character of Rosaline plays no part in the play. Shakespeare wants the audience's attention to be focused solely on Romeo and Juliet. To introduce Rosaline and develop Romeo's relationship with her on stage would be to distract the audience from the main love story.

County count

bound bound to keep the peace (following the quarrel in Act I.1)

reckoning reputation

suit wooing, request to marry

hopes hopes for the future, that is, children

My will ... but a part my desire for her to agree is only part of the matter (Paris has to get Juliet's consent as well)

she agreed when once she has agreed

within ... choice according to what she chooses

according agreeing

accustomed customary, traditional

store company

Earth-treading stars young ladies so beautiful they seem to be stars that have come down to earth

Inherit receive

mine my daughter (Juliet)

May stand ... none may count as one of the crowd though amongst so many hardly noticeable, and not equal to the others ('reckoning' meaning both 'counting' and 'assessment')

sirrah a word used by gentlemen to their inferiors

trudge walk (without the sense of weary effort the word has in modern English)

stay wait

It is written ... nets (proverbs) you should stick to what you know how to do. But the servant muddles them all up

But I am sent ... here writ literacy at this date was confined to the professions and some of the upper classes

holp helped

cures ... another's languish is cured by languishing for someone else (or, perhaps, by making someone else languish)

plantain leaf Romeo takes the 'infection' of line 49 literally, and so wittily suggests a herbal remedy; plantain, a common English weed was used to cure infection and staunch blood

God gi' good-e'en God give you good evening

crush drink

Rosaline the first time Romeo's beloved is named

unattainted unprejudiced, impartial

these these eyes of mine

poised balanced, weighed

scant scarcely

my own my own as belonging to my lady

SCENE 3   **Juliet is prepared by her mother to look out for Paris at the party**

Time: later on Sunday afternoon (I.3.81)

Constantly interrupted by the Nurse, Lady Capulet tells Juliet that Paris wants to marry her, and advises her to take careful note of how handsome he is at the feast that night. Juliet agrees to see if she likes him.

In this, Juliet's first appearance, she is submissive and obedient to her parents (see especially lines 98–100); when she has fallen in love she will discover a new independence of mind. The Nurse's words at the opening of this scene are echoed when (with very different consequences) Lady Capulet again sends her to fetch Juliet in IV.5.1–4.

by my maidenhead ... twelve the implication is that by thirteen the Nurse had no maidenhead to swear by

God forbid that is, God forbid that anything should have happened to her as she does not come

give leave awhile leave us alone for a while

thou's ... counsel thou shalt hear our private talk

teen sorrow

Lammastide 1 August, a harvest festival

odd a few (in the next line the Nurse takes the word in its modern sense)

Susan the Nurse's daughter

earthquake earthquakes were regarded by Elizabethan's as ominous portents

wormwood a bitter-tasting plant

dug nipple; the Nurse suckled Juliet (it was common for noble ladies to have 'wet nurses' for their babies); the wormwood was to wean the baby

I ... brain I can remember

fool used as a term of affection here

Shake ... dovehouse the Nurse personifies the dovehouse and its reaction to the earthquake

trow believe

To bid me trudge to tell me to go (because of the earthquake)

high-lone all alone, by herself

th'rood the cross of Christ

'A he

fall backward a bawdy suggestion that when she is older Juliet will lie on her back under a man

holidam holiness; a common exclamation

it stinted she stopped

it ... it she ... her

stone testicle

dispositions the sense is singular, disposition, inclination

man of wax a model, that is, perfect man

married lineament harmonious feature (of his face)

one ... content each suits the other, so making a perfect whole

margent margin; throughout this speech Lady Capulet compares Paris's face to a book

only lacks a cover needs only the embrace of a wife (as 'cover' of his 'book')

The fish ... hide the sense is that just as fish live in the sea so a fair man (Paris) needs a fair wife (Juliet)

bigger i.e., when pregnant

endart dart, pierce

Nurse cursed the Nurse is cursed (for not being there to help)

in extremity in dire need of help

wait serve at table

straight straightaway, immediately

happy ... days the Nurse thinks of the sexual joy with which a married woman can end the day

SCENE 4 **Romeo's misgivings about attending the Capulet party are overcome by Mercutio**

Time: Sunday evening (I.2.20, 81–100; I.3.81)

Romeo, his cousin Benvolio and his friend Mercutio – a kinsman of the Prince (III.1.109, 145, 188–9; V.3.295) who now appears for the first time – discuss whether to go into Capulet's feast. Although Benvolio and Romeo have not been invited – Mercutio is included amongst the guests on the servant's list (I.2.64–9) – it was quite usual for uninvited maskers to join such parties, and Benvolio is all for going in. Romeo, however, does not care to dance, and, because of a dream, fears something awful – perhaps even his death – will result if they do go in. But Mercutio makes light of his fears, and they enter.

This scene adds little to the action, but it introduces a note of foreboding just as Romeo is to meet Juliet for the first time, and it introduces the important character of Mercutio.

maskers people wearing masks on their faces; although *masked balls* (or dances), fashionable at this time, should not be confused with *masques*, dramatic entertainments involving music and dancing, improvised masques could easily be presented by people in masks and costumes at such a party as Capulet's

What ... our excuse shall we introduce ourselves and excuse our intrusion; it was customary for maskers to present themselves, often with a formal speech – see, for example, Shakespeare's *Love's Labour's Lost*, V.2.158–69, and *Henry VIII*, Act I.4.65–72

The date ... prolixity such speeches ('prolixity') are out of fashion ('date')

Cupid maskers would often send a boy, dressed as Cupid, to introduce them – see, for example, Shakespeare's *Timon of Athens*, Act I.2.117–22

hoodwinked blindfolded

Tartar's ... of lath Cupid's wooden bow, from which he loosed his arrows of love, was shaped like a lip, unlike the curved English bow; Shakespeare thought this may have been a Tartar shape from central Asia (although it is in fact Grecian) or, more probably, used 'Tartar' vaguely to mean 'Eastern'

crowkeeper scarecrow

without-book memorised

measure us ... will judge us as they like

measure them a measure dance one dance for them

torch torchbearers would not join in the dancing

ambling dancing (a contemptuous term)

stakes fixes

bound ... bound ... bound (pun) height ... tied ... leap

pitch height

case mask

A visor for a visor mask for an ugly face

quote notice

betake his legs take to his legs in dancing

rushes these were strewn on the floor

proverbed ... phrase supported (in what I wish to do) by an old proverb that the onlooker sees the best of the game

game that is, here, dancing

ne'er so fair never so good (as now); there was a proverbial saying that one should leave the game (gambling) when the game was at its best

dun's the mouse a quibble on 'done' in line 39; because the mouse is dark ('dun') it is not easily seen, and so, the meaning is 'be quiet', and so unnoticed like the mouse

constable's own word the constable, or policeman, would bid his companions be quiet when waiting to catch a criminal

Dun a name for a horse; there was an expression 'Dun in the mire', like the modern 'stick-in-the-mud', someone who will not venture on anything new

burn daylight waste time; Romeo takes Mercutio literally in the next line

Take ... meaning take the sense of what I say, don't take me literally

for our ... wits for good sense is five times more apparent in what we mean than in what we say (that is, than in the words which are the result of what we learn through our five senses)

tonight last night

in bed asleep in line 51 Mercutio used 'lie' in the sense 'tell an untruth'; Romeo takes it in the sense 'lie down'

Queen Mab queen of the fairies

agate a precious stone, often engraved and set in rings

atomies tiny creatures

spinners spiders

traces reins

film fine thread of cobweb

Pricked ... maid there was a saying that, when maids were idle, worms grew in their fingers

suit petition (which a courtier would present to the king for a fee)

tithe-pig a pig due to the parish priest who received the tenth part (or 'tithe') of the agricultural produce of his parish

benefice position in the church held by a parish priest, for which he received payment

ambuscados ambushes

Spanish blades Spain was famous for the quality of its swords

healths drinks (from the expression 'drink to your health')

bakes matts, tangles together in a hard lump

elf-locks tangled hair was thought to be the work of elves; to untangle it would bring bad luck (line 91)

sluttish very dirty

hag wicked, ugly fairy

learns ... bear teaches them first how to bear children; Mercutio in fact means 'teach them how to conceive children' for he is thinking of young women dreaming of sex as a result of Mab's influence

carriage both 'deportment' and 'the carrying of a child in the womb'

from ourselves from our purpose

date time

expire the term complete the allotted span

SCENE 5   Romeo and Juliet meet for the first time and fall in love

Time: later Sunday evening (I.2.20, 81–100; I.3.81)

In Capulet's house the servants are busy clearing the hall for the dance to follow the meal. Capulet welcomes the maskers and watches the dance, recollecting with his cousin his own dancing days long ago. Tybalt realises that one of the maskers is a Montague, and is furious at the intrusion. Capulet, identifying Romeo, orders Tybalt to control himself and behave civilly to so fine a youth, but Tybalt resolves that this will not be the end of the matter. Romeo, who does not take part in the dance, has noticed Juliet and is overpowered by her beauty. He approaches her when the dance ends and in the fourteen lines of an English **sonnet** he woos her, they fall in love and kiss. The Nurse interrupts them, and the scene ends with Romeo learning that Juliet is a Capulet, she that Romeo is a Montague – that is, that each loves an enemy.

> Building on the last lines of I.4, this scene deepens the note of foreboding. The audience is painfully aware of the hostility and resentment surrounding Romeo and Juliet. Their first encounter is thus fraught with the potential for tragedy.

take away clear away

trencher wooden plate

joint stools wooden stools

court-cupboard sideboard

marchpane marzipan

let ... Nell the servants are to have their own party; Susan and Nell would be their guests

longer liver (colloquialism) Death, who will take us all in the end, so let us be merry now

walk a bout have a dance

makes dainty is coy (in refusing to dance for no very good reason)

Am I ... ye does what I say affect you

A hall clear the room, let us have a hall

knaves the servants (the word is used in good humour here)

turn the tables up in order to clear the room for dancing

unlooked-for because Romeo and his friends were not expected

Pentecost Whitsun

ward youth under twenty-one years of age

Ethiop Ethiopian, strictly, though the word was used of any Negro

shows appears

The measure done when the dance has ended

rude rough (physically) and coarse (socially)

should must

slave not literally, but a term of contempt

antic face fantastic or grotesque mask

fleer sneer

solemnity celebration

stock parentage, the noble line of a family's descent

portly dignified

well-governed well mannered

patient calm (Capulet does not mean that Tybalt should be patient and wait for another opportunity)

ill-beseeming semblance unsuitable appearance

goodman a term used to address a yeoman, that is, a person below the rank of gentleman and so an insult to Tybalt (especially when coupled with 'boy')

Go to an expression of exasperation

mutiny disturbance

You ... cock-a-hoop a colloquial expression explained by Capulet's following ironic 'You'll be the man!'

saucy insolent (the word was then stronger in sense than in modern English)

contrary contradict

hearts friends (Capulet turns aside to address his guests)

perforce compelled

wilful eager, determined

seeming apparently

If I profane... effect I take in these lines, which make up a **sonnet** Shakespeare pursues an elaborate religious **conceit** (or extended image), likening Romeo's approach to Juliet to that of a pilgrim to the shrine of a saint, and a kiss to a prayer; such use of religious imagery was not unusual in love poetry, but the delicate ingenuity and detail of this example are remarkable; it has added point in that Romeo's name means, in Italian, 'pilgrim to Rome'

mannerly proper

saints that is, statues of saints

palmer a pilgrim who carried a palm leaf to show he had been to Jerusalem; here, a play on the palm of the hand

though grant ... sake though they grant what is prayed for, that is, they are 'moved' (persuaded) by prayers, they do not move physically

by th'book Juliet either admits she is deeply affected by the kiss, or she draws back and covers her feelings, for the phrase may mean either 'expertly' ('you have learned how') or 'formally' ('you kiss as though following written instructions, without feeling')

chinks money (because Juliet is the Capulet heir)

dear account awful reckoning to pay

My life ... debt indebted to, dependent on, my foe

banquet not the main meal, which was cleared away for the dance, but a light supper

fay faith

waxes grows

Prodigious ominous, monstrous

ACT II

SCENE 1   Though mocked by his friends, Romeo cannot bear to leave Juliet's house

Time: Sunday night, immediately after Capulet's party (II.1.3–4)

After the Chorus has summarised the situation, stressing the fact that Romeo and Juliet cannot easily meet because of their families' feud, Romeo enters for a moment, and we hear that he cannot bear to leave the house where Juliet lives. He withdraws as Benvolio and Mercutio enter looking for him. Benvolio thinks he has seen Romeo jump over a wall (which, we learn in II.2, surrounds the Capulet house and garden) and Mercutio, who does not know Romeo now loves Juliet, attempts to provoke him to rejoin them by making fun of, and bawdy remarks about, Romeo's love for Rosaline. But Romeo does not return and the two friends go home to bed without him.

This pause in the action increases the audience's expectation of the lovers' next meeting. The parting from his friends enacts the isolation of Romeo and his separation from the familiar world which is the lot of both lovers in the play.

Chorus now usually omitted in performances since it adds nothing to the action, although it does add intensity to the love plot

old desire i.e., Romeo's love for Rosaline

young affection i.e., Romeo's new love for Juliet

fair fair woman (Rosaline)

matched compared

supposed although supposed his enemy as a Capulet, Juliet is not his foe

use to are accustomed to

Tempering extremities modifying extremely harsh circumstances

extreme sweet excess of love

go forward that is, go forward beyond Juliet's house (and so away from her)

dull earth Romeo's own body (God created Adam from earth)

centre three senses combine: (i) earth was thought to be a heavy element which tended down to the centre of the world (because of gravitation, though that was not then understood), and so Romeo, as earth, must go to his centre; (ii) the centre of Romeo's world is Juliet, as she is all to him; (iii) the heart is the centre of man, and, as Juliet has Romeo's heart, he must return to her to find his centre: the sense of all these meanings is that Romeo cannot leave Juliet, the centre of his life

orchard probably garden, rather than literally an orchard (though this one does have fruit trees in it, see II.2. 108)

conjure to call up spirits by reciting magic words (Mercutio goes on to make fun of Romeo's love by reciting a mock incantation, made up of lovers' protestations)

gossip Venus familiar friend Venus, the goddess of love and mother of Cupid

purblind blind

Abraham Cupid two senses are possible: (i) the cunning and roguish Cupid, naked but for a loin cloth, is like the 'Abraham men', half-naked beggars and thieves who wandered England – so, 'rascally Cupid'; (ii) the patriarch Abraham in the Old Testament lived to be 175 years old, and Cupid, though a child, was an old god – so 'old Cupid'

trim accurately

King Cophetua the hero of an old ballad who fell in love with a beggar girl; the point of the allusion is that this was an unlikely match, and so Cupid was particularly clever to bring it about

ape is dead a term of affection; Mercutio means that as Romeo pretends to be dead by not appearing, his ghost must be conjured up

demesnes domains, that is, Rosaline's sexual parts

raise conjure up

circle conjurors worked in a magic circle, but in these lines there is a second bawdy sense, with references to the female ('circle') and aroused male sexual parts ('raise', 'stand'), to the sexual act ('laid') and its aftermath ('down')

consorted accompanied

humorous humid and (with reference to Romeo's apparent unfriendliness) moody

medlar soft, pear-shaped indented fruit, thought to resemble a woman's sexual parts (with a pun on 'meddle', meaning 'to make love')

open-arse dialect name for medlar, and a reference to a sexually available female body

poppering pear a kind of pear and a pun on the act of love-making

truckle bed a small bed, such as a child might use, implying that Mercutio is innocently going to his bed, while Romeo indulges in sexual activity

SCENE 2   **Romeo and Juliet avow their love despite their families' hostility and Romeo resolves to seek the Friar's assistance to effect their marriage**

Time: Sunday night, immediately following II.1, to dawn on Monday (II.2.1, 176, 188–91)

Romeo dismisses Mercutio's jokes, and, seeing Juliet at her balcony, adores her beauty. Juliet, not knowing Romeo is below, confesses that she loves him despite the fact that he is a Montague. Romeo speaks to her and, although Juliet is afraid for his life, he remains in the garden and they acknowledge their love. Juliet speaks honestly and frankly of her affection, and freely tells Romeo that if he means what he says and can send word the next day how they may be married, she will readily be his wife. She arranges to send a go-between to Romeo by nine in the morning to learn what plan he has made. When she goes in, Romeo decides to go to see his father confessor, Friar Laurence, for advice on how to bring about the marriage.

The love theme of the first part of the play now begins to move quickly to its climax. Although Romeo and Juliet have only just met, by the time the crucial meeting we now see is over, they are planning to marry. It is for the remarkably beautiful treatment of the confession of love in this scene that the play is best remembered. (The quality of the love here celebrated is emphasised by the contrast with Mercutio's bawdy innuendo in the previous scene.)

He jests ... wound someone who has never been hurt makes light of another's scars: Romeo means that as Mercutio has never been in love he can easily laugh at a lover's sorrows; 'wounded' recalls Cupid and his arrows

Be not her maid Romeo has likened Juliet to the sun; in not wanting her to be the maid of the virgin goddess of the moon, Diana, he confesses his hope she may accept his love and so cease to be a virgin

vestal livery spotlessly pure costume

fools that is, those who remain virgin and unmarried

spheres in the old astronomy of Ptolemy the stars and planets were thought to revolve around the earth as though in round, transparent tubes, called 'spheres'

they that is, the stars

wherefore why; that is, why are you Romeo and a Montague rather than a member of some other family?

though not even if you were not

owes owns

thee dislike offends, displeases, you

the place death to be in this place is to risk your life

proof protected against, immune

but thou unless you, if you do not

wanting of if I lacked

Fain would ... form gladly would I follow custom (which requires that the woman refuses her lover's address)

compliment conventional polite manners, formality: Juliet's determination here to speak plainly of her love, though hardly what would be expected of a young girl alone at night with a man, is a key feature of her character; it contrasts very obviously with Romeo's elaborate imagery (which Juliet interrupts at 1.109)

Jove king of the gods in Roman mythology

So thou wilt if that will make you

fond affectionate and foolish

cunning ... strange skill to be aloof or distant, that is, to follow the usual rules of courtship

frank generous

bent intention, inclination

strife urging

Love ... love a loved one ... a loved one

tassel-gentle tercel-gentle, a male falcon, the most prized by falconers (and so a compliment to Romeo)

Bondage is hoarse as a young girl Juliet would not be free to leave the house unaccompanied or to meet a man without a chaperone; hence, she is 'bound' and cannot call out to Romeo for fear of discovery

Echo a mythical nymph condemned to repeat the last words anyone spoke to her, who, unable to declare her love for Narcissus, lived alone in a cave until she died of a broken heart, leaving only her voice behind

nyas a young hawk which has not yet left the nest to fly (and so Romeo's fitting reply to 'tassel-gentle')

wanton mischievous child

gyves shackles

Titan's wheels in Greek mythology the Titan sun god Hyperion rode across the sky in a chariot

ghostly spiritual

dear hap dear happening, that is, good fortune

SCENE 3   Friar Laurence agrees to arrange the secret marriage

Time: early Monday morning, immediately following II.2 (II.2.188–93; II.3.1–4, 28–30, 38)

Romeo visits Friar Laurence, who is glad to hear Romeo is no longer infatuated with Rosaline, but astonished to learn that another woman has taken her place. Nevertheless, he agrees to help arrange the marriage, as this may serve to unite the families of Montague and Capulet (note that this is the only justification for the Friar's willingness to assist in a secret marriage).

The Friar, like the Prince, Escalus, is anxious to end the feud. With the Church (the Friar) and the State (the Prince) both trying to heal old wounds, it is the more tragic that the love of Romeo and Juliet should be destroyed by this very quarrel and that only their deaths can bring about the reconciliation which the Friar here hopes their marriage will achieve.

The Friar's long opening **soliloquy** establishes him as kindly and good-natured and a man skilled in the poisons and medicines that may be made from plants. We are thus prepared to accept that he could make the potion he later gives to Juliet. More than this, the Friar's vision of the world as potentially good and evil underlines one of the main themes of the play: love and hate are very close, as poison and medicine may be derived from one plant, and should hate predominate, love will be destroyed. Some texts bring Romeo in at line 19, so that he overhears the last part of the speech: it is certainly true that the final lines of the speech are an unintentional prophecy of Romeo's fate, for he will die of poison because of the circumstances brought about by the hatred of Montagues and Capulets.

osier cage willow basket

baleful poisonous

None but for some there is no plant which does not have some good qualities

mickle great

stones rocks, in the sense of 'minerals'

to the earth that is, to the inhabitants of the earth

strained forced away, perverted

Revolts ... abuse turns away from its true nature if it is abused

with that part by means of that part (the nose, which smells the plant) revives ('cheers') the other parts of the body

And where ... plant the Friar here compares the spiritual state of man to the natural state of plants: as poison and medicine are found in one plant, so man has good and evil in him ('grace and rude will'); if the evil ('the worser')

predominates, then the man is consumed by wickedness and spiritual death ('the canker death') overtakes him

Benedicite (Latin) 'May you be blessed'

argues ... head shows a disturbed mind

good morrow goodbye

unbruised unharmed by the world, that is, innocent

unstuffed not filled with troubles

distemperature uneasiness of mind

one hath wounded ... wounded that is, I fell in love with one who loves me; the wounds derive from Cupid's arrow. An apt image here as Juliet is Romeo's 'enemy'

I ... hatred that is, such as might be expected if one has been wounded by an enemy

steads helps

homely unsophisticated, that is, plain, straightforward

pass go along

Jesu Maria Jesus son of Mary

sentence saying, maxim

Thy love ... spell your expressions of love were as though recited ('read') by memory ('rote') by someone who could not understand ('spell') what he had learned to say: these comments point to the conventional and very ornate language Romeo has used to describe his feelings; unlike Juliet, who speaks plainly, as the Friar would wish, Romeo always uses the literary terms and images of Elizabethan love poetry

In one respect because of one thing

stand on insist on, or, depend on

SCENE 4   Preparations are made for the secret marriage

Time: 12 noon on Monday (II.4.110)

Benvolio and Mercutio, who went home to bed at the end of II.1 without finding Romeo, are still looking for him the next morning. We hear from them that Tybalt has carried out his threat (I.5.91–2) not to ignore the matter of Romeo's intrusion into Capulet's party and has sent a challenge to Montague, which Benvolio believes Romeo will accept. When Romeo enters (coming from his meeting with the Friar) he is in good spirits (for the first time in the play) and engages in witty exchanges with Mercutio. In

II.2.167–9 Juliet had arranged to send a messenger to Romeo, and now the Nurse comes. Romeo tells her to arrange for Juliet to go to confession that afternoon and says they will then be married by the Friar. He also arranges for his servant to give the Nurse a rope ladder, by means of which he will enter Juliet's room that night. The Nurse agrees to these plans.

Tybalt's behaviour is ominously at odds with the love that has developed in the previous scenes. Its introduction at this point, as Romeo and Juliet are preparing to escape from their families' hostility, creates a sense of unease which undercuts the exhilaration of Romeo's mood and the apparent progress of the lovers towards marriage. The happiness which they expect to result is already in jeopardy.

answer accept the challenge, though Mercutio jokingly takes it in its usual sense in the next line

how he dares saying that he dares to fight

already dead that is, through the sufferings of love

pin centre

blind bow-boy's butt-shaft Cupid's blunt arrow

Prince of Cats Tybalt's name was given to the cat in the old medieval story of Reynard the Fox

He fights ... *hay* Mercutio mocks Tybalt as a duellist skilled only with the slender, pointed Italian rapier, which pierces but does not cut the opponent; duels with such weapons only became fashionable in England in the 1590s, and were scorned by those, like Mercutio, who held that the heavier English sword, with its sharp edge to slash opponents, was the weapon for a real fight, requiring strength and valour

as ... pricksong as you sing carefully following printed music, that is, according to the rules

rests ... rests observes every detail of the music

butcher ... button because the rapier hits only a small point and does not cause a great wound like a sword

duellist the first use of the word in English literature; Mercutio uses it in scorn

first house finest school of duelling

cause ... *hay* these are all duelling terms

The pox of a plague on

antic grotesque

affecting fantasticoes affected fops

new tuners followers of every new fashion, who affect the latest idioms and forms of speech (Mercutio goes on to give examples)

pardon-me a new and over-used phrase among courtiers of the time (in Mercutio's view, a hypocritical phrase)

who stand ... bench Mercutio's usual wordplay: who insist ('stand') so much on the new code of manners ('form') that they cannot tolerate ('sit') the old ways ('bench')

roe several senses are combined: (i) the spawn of a fish, so 'unmanned'; (ii) a kind of deer, so 'without his dear one'; (iii) first syllable of Romeo's name, and so 'only half himself'

numbers verses

Petrarch ... Laura the famous medieval Italian poet Petrarch wrote of his love for Laura, and established many of those literary conventions and images which Elizabethan poets (and Romeo) still used

Dido ... Thisbe all famous women and lovers celebrated in Classical literature; that all their love affairs ended tragically strikes an ominous note

hildings worthless women

slop loose breeches (Romeo has not been to bed, and so has not changed since the party)

gave ... counterfeit deceived us

bow in the hams Mercutio takes 'courtesy' in line 49 as 'curtsey', and suggests Romeo spent the night bending his legs in lovemaking to Rosaline

Meaning, to curtsey ... broad goose now that he has arranged the marriage Romeo is in much better spirits and, for the first time in the play, is Mercutio's equal in wit: in these exchanges they play a number of word games: (i) courtesy, curtsey, courteous (lines 53–6); (ii) pink ('perfection', a flower and an ornament on a shoe, lines 56–9); (iii) pump (a shoe), sole (of a shoe), solely singular (uniquely remarkable), single-soled (weak), solely (only) and singleness (silliness, lines 59–65); (iv) wild goose-chase (a horse race in which all follow the leader, and so, a pointless chase), wild-goose (silly person), goose (prostitute and jester), cooked goose that needs sweetening (apple sauce) and broad goose (rude jester, lines 70–85)

Swits switch, riding crop or whip

cheverel kind of leather that stretches easily

ell measure of forty-five inches

natural idiot

bauble decorated stick, and a bawdy expression for penis

occupy the argument deal with the subject

gear matter

a sail Romeo means that he sees some one coming, as the look-out on a ship would cry 'a sail' when he sighted another ship

shirt and a smock a man and a woman

prick point, but the clock-hand is 'bawdy' because 'prick' also means 'penis'

noon Juliet's go-between was supposed to arrive by 9 a.m. (II.2. 167–9), and Juliet had sent the Nurse on time (II.5.1); she has obviously been distracted from her purpose – that she should be late is entirely characteristic

can … Romeo a rather strange question, since she had met Romeo the night before at the party (Act I.5.112–18, 134–6)

confidence confidential, private conversation

endite invite

bawd woman who keeps a brothel; in what follows Mercutio is bawdy and rude, but not too mistaken about the Nurse's earthy nature

hare slang for a prostitute

lenten pie as no meat was supposed to be eaten during Lent, a hare pie would go stale

hoar mouldy, and a pun on 'whore'

merchant fellow (a term of derision)

ropery bawdy jokes

stand to maintain, carry out

Jacks insolent fellows

flirt-gills loose, immoral women

skains-mates villainous companions

weak contemptible

tackled stair rope ladder

topgallant summit

convoy conveyance

quit thy pains reward your efforts

Two … away a proverb meaning that two can keep a secret, but not three

prating chattering

lay knife aboard a saying meaning 'to lay claim to'

versal universal, whole

dog's name because when pronounced 'R' sounds like a dog's growl (the Nurse is illiterate)

sententious the Nurse (who quite often misuses words) means 'sentence', a saying

apace quickly

SCENE 5   **Juliet learns the arrangements for the marriage**

Time: early Monday afternoon, immediately following II.4 (II.4.110; II.5.1–11)

Juliet waits impatiently and anxiously for the return of the Nurse, who has been gone for three hours. When the Nurse does return, it is only after repeated questions that Juliet learns that Romeo has arranged the marriage for that afternoon.

This short scene achieves dramatic effect from the most unlikely material. The plot requires that Romeo's message is conveyed to Juliet, but, rather than a briefly uninteresting scene in which it is immediately delivered, the garrulousness of the Nurse builds the tension as the audience is made to wait, its impatience growing with Juliet's. The simple delivery of a message thus involves us in sympathy with Juliet, irritation and amusement at the Nurse, and relief when the plan is finally made known. That the scene ends with Juliet speaking of 'high fortune' is ominous: in tragedy, it is when at the height of good fortune that the protagonist is mostly likely to fall.

That's not so That cannot be

nimble pinioned swift-winged

draw love pull the chariot of the goddess of love, Venus

bandy strike a ball (see the previous line)

feign ... dead seem to be dead (because they move so slowly)

leave peace

jaunce jaunt, walk

stay the circumstance wait for the details

simple silly

hot impatient, passionate

coil bother

hie hurry

bird's nest that is, Juliet's room

SCENE 6   Romeo and Juliet are married

Time: later Monday afternoon (II.4.176–82; II.5.66–9)

In an unexpectedly quiet climax to the first movement of the play Romeo and Juliet meet at the Friar's cell and go in to be married.

> By not presenting the marriage on stage, Shakespeare ensures that the memorable scenes will be the lovers' declaration of love (II.2) and their deaths (V.3). Thus, he gives a starkly simple design to the play. Our experience of it in the theatre is of sudden love and sudden death. The marriage seems, and is made by Shakespeare to seem, almost unimportant beside the love itself. The poetic and dramatic affirmation of love is the lover's exchange in II.2; the formal marriage is but a consequence of that.

> By ending this movement of the play so quietly, Shakespeare achieves an obvious contrast with the violence that follows in the next scene: the idyllic, quiet, secret world of love is shattered by Tybalt. The Friar's opening words are cruelly **ironic** in view of what does happen later, and his words at lines 9–11 tragically prophetic.

what sorrow can whatever sorrows can

Too swift … too slow love that is too passionate ('too swift') is as fallible as love that is too cold ('too slow')

Will … flint Juliet walks so lightly her feet seem hardly to touch the ground and so will not wear out the rock ('flint')

gossamers cobwebs

idles drift

vanity the pleasures of the world; the Friar for a moment sadly remembers that, from the point of view of religion, such love is insubstantial

As much … much Romeo's 'thanks' for Juliet's 'good evening' to the Friar (probably a kiss) will be too great a return for a single greeting and so she must include Romeo in it ('as much to him')

and that and since

either each other

Conceit imagination: the plain-speaking Juliet refuses Romeo's invitation to 'blazon' their love in fine phrases

I … wealth I cannot add up ('sum') the total of half my wealth

ACT III

Mercutio's death at the hands of Tybalt is avenged by
Romeo who is then exiled from Verona

Time: Monday afternoon, an hour after the marriage (III.1.112–3)

Mercutio and Benvolio are walking in Verona. Mercutio rejects Benvolio's
suggestion that they should leave the streets as the Capulets are also out-
of-doors and playfully mocks Benvolio's attempt to prevent any fighting by
characterising him as extraordinarily quarrelsome. Mercutio is in fact
describing his own character, for when they meet Tybalt Mercutio
deliberately provokes him. Tybalt, however, is looking for Romeo, and,
when he enters, Tybalt turns to him and insults him. We know that Tybalt
is infuriated by Romeo's intrusion at Capulet's party but, to Romeo, newly
married to Tybalt's cousin Juliet (and so now related to Tybalt himself),
there seems to be no good reason to quarrel. Mercutio is dismayed by what
he takes to be Romeo's cowardice in refusing to fight, and he himself draws
his sword on Tybalt. As Romeo tries to stop them fighting, Mercutio is
fatally wounded by Tybalt. In a moment of grim foresight, Romeo sees that
this death will cause much sorrow in days to come, but, nevertheless, to
avenge his friend's death, he fights and kills Tybalt. Benvolio persuades
Romeo to flee, since the Prince has decreed that anyone guilty of further
fighting will be punished by death (I.1.96–7). However, because Tybalt has
himself committed a murder, the Prince does not order Romeo's execution,
but exiles him from Verona.

> Thus, in the scene immediately following the marriage, the event
> which will part the lovers occurs. It is the pivotal scene of the play, on
> which the fortune of the protagonists turns. Throughout the second
> act the lovers' fortunes have been steadily improving: Romeo and
> Juliet exchanged vows in II.2; in II.3 the Friar agreed to marry them;
> in II.4 Romeo was in high spirits and told the Nurse of his plan; and
> in II.6 the marriage was accomplished. Now, in a moment, the
> movement towards tragedy (of which we had hints in I.4.106–111;
> I.5.91–2; II.4.6–9, and for which the Chorus has prepared us) begins.
> It is sadly **ironic** that Romeo himself does his best to prevent it: it is
> the misguided sense of honour of his friend, Mercutio, which brings
> it about.

> **Capels** Capulets
> **operation** effect

drawer waiter

hot impetuous

two Mercutio's wordplay on Benvolio's 'to' in line 14

addle as an egg bad as a rotten egg

fee simple full title

for an hour ... quarter before an hour and a quarter had passed; Benvolio means that were he as quarrelsome as Mercutio he would be killed in a fight within this time; it is dramatically **ironic** that Mercutio will be killed within this time because of his quarrelsomeness

Consort ... minstrels Tybalt in line 44 meant 'associate with' by 'consortest', but 'a company of musicians was called a 'consort' and Mercutio sees this as an opportunity to take offence since 'minstrel' (a hired musician) was a term of abuse

fiddlestick i.e., his sword

livery Mercutio, still looking for grievances, takes 'man'in line 55 as 'servant' and exclaims that Romeo does not wear the uniform ('livery') of one of Tybalt's hired men

worship honour; a polite form of address here used ironically by Mercutio, who means that Romeo is Tybalt's servant, or follower, only in the sense that he will follow him to the place for a duel ('field')

excuse ... rage excuse me from showing the appropriate rage

devise guess

tender value

Alla stoccata a duelling term which Mercutio sarcastically uses as a name for Tybalt

as ... me depending on how you treat me

dry-beat cudgel, beat without drawing blood

pilcher scabbard

bandying fighting

sped slain

villain a term of address to a servant, not here implying bad qualities, as it does in Tybalt's use to the gentleman Romeo in line 60, to which Romeo refers in line 125

grave man a serious man and a man in a grave; an appropriate, and moving, jest from the dying Mercutio, who has not once been serious in the play

peppered killed

book of arithmetic book of rules

worms' meat i.e., a corpse

ally relative

cousin relative, through his marriage to Juliet

effeminate like a woman, i.e., unmanly (the distinction between robust manhood and soft womanhood was conventional)

temper character

aspired risen to

on more ... depend portends ill fortune on more days to come: this, and the following line, marked out as a **couplet**, signal the beginning of the tragedy

respective lenity leniency or mildness which is respectful (to Tybalt, as Juliet's, and now, Romeo's, relative)

conduct conductor, guide

This i.e., Romeo's sword

up aroused

amazed bewildered, dazed (a stronger word in Elizabethan English than it is now)

discover reveal

unlucky manage unfortunate handling

true faithful to your word

nice petty, trivial

urged ... displeasure that is, tried to dissuade Tybalt from fighting by reminding him of the Prince's decree against feuding: Benvolio biases his account in Romeo's favour for, although Romeo did 'speak Tybalt fair', he had not mentioned the Prince's displeasure; there is thus some truth in Lady Capulet's later remark, lines 176–7

unruly spleen ungovernable bad temper

but that so that

Retorts returns

envious hostile

newly entertained only just thought of

His fault... end in killing Tybalt Romeo had only anticipated the law, which would have condemned Tybalt to death for murdering Mercutio

My blood the blood of my family (as Mercutio was his relative)

amerce punish by a fine

mine my relative

purchase out buy off, obliterate

attend our will take heed of what I command

Mercy ... kill if the law is merciful to murderers then it simply encourages further murders

SCENE *2*   News of Tybalt's death and Romeo's banishment is brought to Juliet

Time: later Monday afternoon, three hours after the marriage (III.2.99) *and two hours after Romeo's fight* (III.1.112–13)

Juliet is waiting impatiently for the night, which will bring Romeo to her (as he had planned before their marriage II.4.183–7; II.5.72–4). In a strikingly dramatic moment, just as Juliet is taken up with joyful thoughts of Romeo and the consummation of their love, the Nurse enters to dash all her hopes by telling her of Tybalt's death and Romeo's banishment. (A very similar technique is used by Shakespeare at the beginning of V.1.) To the Nurse's surprise, after a moment's shock at what Romeo has done, Juliet is not appalled that he has killed her cousin Tybalt, but full of grief at his banishment. The scene ends with the Nurse agreeing to bring Romeo from Friar Laurence's cell, where he has hidden since the fight.

This is a scene of **tragic irony**. As it opens, the audience, which already knows of Tybalt's death, is aware that what is, in effect, Juliet's wedding hymn will lead to no such happiness as she anticipates. When Juliet herself comes to realise that the wedding night is now to be the lovers' farewell, she speaks **metaphorically** of this parting as her death, darkening the atmosphere of the play and, unknowingly, alerting the audience to her fate. Juliet's vulnerability is underscored by the audience's prior knowledge of what has occurred, and its realisation of what will occur.

Gallop ... Phoebus' lodging Juliet is referring to the horses pulling the sun god's chariot across the sky, i.e., she wants sunset to arrive quickly
Phaëton Phoebus allowed his son Phaëton to drive his chariot, who was unable to prevent it racing too near the earth and was destroyed by a thunderbolt from Zeus lest the world be consumed by fire
close enclosing, concealing
runaway's a famous crux (that is, a textual passage which puzzles commentators): who it is that is a 'runaway' is not clear, but the general sense is that the lovers will be safe in the darkness, free from spies

civil decorous, gentle

lose ... match Juliet must yield her body to Romeo ('lose') and so win a husband

Hood ... blood Juliet is asking the night to hide ('hood') her blushes ('blood') as she yields her virginity, but the image, from falconry, is appropriate in other ways: the head of an untrained ('unmanned') falcon was covered with a hood until it grew used to its owner (or 'man'); Juliet is untrained in the ways of love-making and 'unmanned' because she has not yet had a man as a lover

bating fluttering

cords ropes (that Romeo had given her, II.4.183–7)

weraday alas

undone ruined

envious full of hostility, malicious

Romeo can the Nurse means that Romeo can be so full of hostility as to kill Tybalt

Or those ... 'Ay' if you must answer 'yes' because those eyes (that is, Romeo's) are shut (that is, he is dead)

God save the mark a common Elizabethan exclamation when something awful or disagreeable was mentioned

corse corpse

swounded swooned

Vile earth that is, her own body

heavy literally, and meaning 'sad'

so contrary in such opposite directions (Juliet thought the Nurse had been describing Romeo's body)

dreadful trumpet in Christian belief the Day of Judgement (Doomsday) will be announced by the sound of a trumpet

serpent when the Devil tempted Eve in Paradise he appeared as a snake ('serpent'): Juliet is, for a moment, appalled that her lover could have done such a thing, and throughout this speech compares his apparently deceptive mildness with the deceptive appearance of the 'fiend' Satan; but when the Nurse agrees that men are all deceivers, Juliet quickly recovers her faith in Romeo

bower enclose, embower

naught wicked

And needly ... ranked must be accompanied

modern ordinary

sound express

wot know

scene 3   The Friar advises the despairing Romeo to flee to Mantua
          while he seeks to reconcile the feuding families and to gain a
          pardon from the Prince

Time: late on Monday evening (III.3.164, 172)

Since killing Tybalt Romeo has hidden in Friar Laurence's cell (III.2.141).
The Friar now tells him that he is banished by the Prince which, as it means
separation from Juliet, is to Romeo only another way of condemning him
to death. The Nurse comes, as she had promised Juliet she would
(III.2.140–1), and her description of Juliet's grief so fills Romeo with guilt
and regret that he tries to kill himself. Horrified at this, the Friar in a long
speech shows Romeo the folly of suicide; tells him that he has much to be
thankful for; urges him to go that night to Juliet, as arranged (II.4.183–7;
II.5.72–4), to comfort her; and then to leave Verona for Mantua, where he
may live until such time as the Friar can publicly proclaim the marriage,
reconcile the families and gain a pardon from the Prince. To all this,
Romeo agrees. The Nurse leaves to tell Juliet that Romeo is coming, and
the scene ends with the Friar warning Romeo to leave Verona with care,
and assuring him that he will keep in touch with him through Romeo's
servant (Balthasar).

This scene balances III.2: that had presented Juliet's reaction to the
news of Tybalt's death and Romeo's banishment; we now see how
Romeo responds to his bad fortune. The Nurse herself parallels them
in III.3.85–6.

parts personal qualities

vanished from escaped from (and so vanished into air)

without outside, beyond

deadly sin the Friar exclaims at what seems to him to be the sin of ingratitude
for what is, legally, mercy, since the Prince could have had Romeo put to
death

Thy fault ... death our law prescribes death for thy fault

rushed a strange word, perhaps a printer's error for 'brushed' or 'thrust'

validity value

Still blush Romeo supposes Juliet's innocence such that her lips will blush for 'kissing' each other when they touch

mean ... mean means ... however distasteful

mangle mutilate, torture

fond foolish

Displant move

prevails not cannot prevail in argument, convince

dispute ... estate discuss the state of your affairs

simpleness folly; Romeo's folly is that he remains lying on the ground (line 70) and will not hide

woeful sympathy Romeo 'sympathises', or identifies, with Juliet in that he behaves exactly like her in his grief (or 'woe')

O the sound of moaning

level aim

sack plunder

ill-beseeming inappropriate, unnatural

tempered formed, balanced

wit intellectual ability

Digressing if it deviates

Killing if it kills

flask container for gunpowder

dead wishing to be dead

mishavèd misbehaved

Watch be set at nightfall the city gates would be closed and a guard ('Watch') set

blaze proclaim

comfort cheerfulness

hap happening

chances occurs

brief with so brief a farewell, that is, hurriedly

SCENE 4   **Lord Capulet arranges a marriage between Juliet and Paris**

Time: night-time, very early Tuesday morning (III.4.5–7, 34–5)

The lovers have not been seen together since the short scene of their marriage (II.6). Since then, in III.2 and III.3 we have seen their separate reactions to the ill-fortune which has intervened, but, before they come together to take their farewell (in what will prove to be their last scene together until their deaths) Shakespeare keeps the audience in anticipation by turning aside for a moment to introduce a new complication, a stroke of fate which is to hasten the tragedy. He had prepared for this in I.2–3 when we learned of Paris's suit for Juliet. Then Capulet had said that he would follow Juliet's wishes in the matter (I.2.16–19), but, now that Tybalt's death has so disturbed the family that he has not been able to discuss it with her, he tells Paris that he is sure Juliet will obey her father and so he goes ahead to arrange the marriage for Thursday without consulting Juliet. His wife, Lady Capulet, is to tell her (not ask her).

There is **dramatic irony** and **tragic irony** in this scene. In view of Juliet's obedience and compliance in I.3 it is no wonder that Capulet is so confident she will obey him now. He is, of course, proved wrong, and the staging of the scene at this moment in the plot underlines this in a dramatically ironic way. There is a contrast implied between this marriage arranged by parents and the marriage, resulting from love, which is about to be consummated in Juliet's room. Juliet has now moved far from I.3; her parents act as though she is still the same girl, but she is now, unknown to them (but not to the audience), a married woman awaiting her bridegroom. At the same time, unknown to the lovers, events are working against their relationship and threatening their love (tragic irony). The audience is in the privileged position of understanding more about Juliet than her parents, and of knowing more about her parents' plans than Juliet.

move persuade

promise assure

mewed ... heaviness shut up with her grief; Juliet's real cause of grief is, of course, not Tybalt's death, as her mother supposes, but Romeo's banishment, and she is shut up in her room only for Romeo to come to her

desperate tender bold offer

keep no great ado not have an elaborate ceremony with many guests

late recently

held him carelessly did not esteem ('held') him dearly

ere you go to bed this introduces a moment's suspense: it was late at night that Romeo left the Friar (III.3.172), and if Lady Capulet goes now to Juliet's

room she will either find Romeo there or be there when he arrives; Lady
Capulet does, in fact, disturb the lovers (III.5.39–40)

against for

SCENE 5   After spending the night together, Romeo and Juliet part.
Juliet refuses to marry Paris

Time: dawn on Tuesday (III.5.1–2, 6–10, 40)

In this, only the fourth scene in which they have been together (I.5, II.2,
II.6), the lovers have to admit that day is dawning and, unless they part,
Romeo will be captured and put to death for not going into exile (as the
Prince had decreed, III.1.194–5). The Nurse interrupts them to say that
Juliet's mother is coming (as she had been told to do by Capulet, III.4.15,
31), and so Romeo leaves. Juliet, filled with misgivings, fears that they will
never meet again. Just as Juliet has bid her husband farewell, she is told by
her mother that in two days she must marry Paris. Lady Capulet says that
Juliet's father has arranged this so as to stop her grieving for Tybalt. He
wants her to have an occasion for joy. Paris himself gives the same
explanation in the next scene (IV.1.9–15), and this would explain why
Capulet went ahead in III.4 without consulting Juliet.

Juliet flatly refuses the marriage and, when her father comes in, he is
furious at this disobedience, shocking both the Nurse and Lady Capulet by
the violence of his anger and the insults he hurls at Juliet. He swears that
unless Juliet obeys him he will never see her again. In comic contrast, the
Nurse happily suggests that Juliet should indeed marry Paris as Romeo is
unlikely ever to be able to return. Juliet is naturally appalled at this, and, as
Romeo had sought out the Friar when he wished to marry Juliet (II.3) and
after killing Tybalt (III.3), so, in this new difficulty, Juliet decides to go to
him for help.

> The play does not depict Romeo's arrival at Juliet's room, only his
> departure. It is another way in which the atmosphere is darkened:
> sorrowful parting, rather than joyous greeting, sets the mood. Juliet's
> fears that she will never again see Romeo similarly strengthen the
> impression that the tragedy is now gathering momentum, as does
> Romeo's remark in line 36 that the lovers' predicament darkens the
> lighter the day becomes. As their parting occurs at dawn, some time

has passed since Romeo left the Friar late on Monday night
(III.3.172). The assumption is that during the night Romeo has been
with Juliet and consummated their marriage. Indeed, it adds to the
irony of III.4 if Romeo is actually with Juliet as her father is arranging
her marriage to Paris. This would mean that the secret love match is
being consummated (and so confirmed emotionally and legally) even
as Capulet plans a public wedding for Juliet. That plan is another
example of tragic irony: hoping to make Juliet happy Capulet in fact
achieves the exact opposite and contributes to those circumstances
which bring about her death.

fearful frightened

envious malicious

exhales draws up; meteors were thought to be drawn up from the earth,
ignited and 'exhaled' by the sun

so if

reflex of Cynthia's brow reflection of the moon (Cynthia was goddess of the
moon)

care desire, concern

sharps musical notes

division music; Juliet puns on the word in the next line

Some ... change eyes the toad, having more beautiful eyes than the lark, was
said to have exchanged his eyes for those of the more attractive lark

hunt's up early morning song to wake huntsmen; as newly married couples
were similarly awakened, the term was used in this context too

be much in years have aged many years

ill-divining soul soul which foresees bad fortune

procures brings

feeling deeply felt: Juliet's mother believes Juliet means the death of Tybalt
when in fact she suffers for the loss of Romeo

friend to Lady Capulet this means Tybalt; to the audience, Romeo

asunder apart

venge avenge

Mantua Lady Capulet cannot possibly know this: Romeo, who has only this
moment left the room, can hardly yet be in Mantua, and, anyway, only the
Friar and (presumably) Juliet know of his plan

runagate renegade

dram small drink; Lady Capulet means poison; ironically, it will be Romeo who poisons himself

dead Juliet is deliberately ambiguous: to her mother she says she wants Romeo dead; her true meaning is that her heart is dead as Romeo has left

temper her mother takes Juliet to mean 'mix'; we take the meaning 'moderate' or 'weaken'

wreak avenge

careful considerate

sorted out arranged

sudden unexpected

in happy time opportunely (ironically said)

he should be he that wants to be

at your hands from you

brother's brother-in-law's (see III.1.146)

conduit water pipe (Juliet is crying)

bark boat

overset overturn

will none will have none of it

Take me with you let me understand you

proud grateful, pleased

bride bridegroom

But thankful ... love but, though I hate what you have arranged, I am grateful to you who intended I should love it

chopped logic hair splitting, quibbling with words

minion worthless girl

fettle groom a horse, that is, get ready, prepare

joints limbs, that is, her body, herself

hurdle sledge on which criminals were dragged to their punishment

green-sickness carrion pallid as a corpse

baggage hussy, good-for-nothing

tallow hard, yellowy fat from which candles were made

Hang thee may you be hanged

My fingers itch that is, I itch to strike her

lent given; in Christian thought all things on earth are but lent during life

hilding worthless girl

rate berate, scold

Prudence probably not the Nurse's real Christian name, but used sarcastically by Capulet

Smatter ... gossips chatter with your friends, and not with me

God ... e'en in bidding her good evening Capulet is telling the Nurse to go

gravity wisdom (Capulet is being ironic)

God's bread the bread blessed in the Holy Communion service

matched married

demesnes estates, lands

puling whining, whimpering

mammet puppet

in her fortune's tender when fortune makes her an offer

an if

Graze feed: Capulet insults Juliet by using a word applied to animals

do not use am not accustomed

Advise consider

Nor what ... good nor shall anything of mine ever help you

be forsworn break my word

a word that is, a word to your father on your behalf

faith vow, that is, her marriage vow

practise stratagems use cunning schemes

all the world to nothing it is a safe bet

challenge claim

dishclout dishcloth

Beshrew ... heart curse me if I'm wrong

Ancient damnation damned old woman

compare comparison

twain two, that is, separated

ACT IV

SCENE 1 The Friar plans to fake Juliet's death

Time: Tuesday (IV.1.90), and, as both Paris and Juliet have come straight to the Friar following conversations at dawn on Tuesday, the morning of that day

In this scene Juliet and her suitor, Paris, meet for the only time in the play. Paris has come to see the Friar to tell him of his planned marriage with Juliet. He explains that the haste is because Capulet wants to lessen his daughter's grief at Tybalt's death. Juliet enters (she had resolved to visit the Friar at the end of III.5), and carefully avoids answering directly Paris's questions about her love for him and their marriage. Paris leaves, thinking Juliet is to confess to the Friar. In fact, she implores his help in avoiding the marriage with Paris. The Friar suggests that the night before her wedding (that is, tomorrow, Wednesday, night) she should take a potion he can give her which will make her appear to be dead but from the effects of which she will awake unharmed, as from a sleep. When she is found on her wedding day, all will think her dead, and she will be placed in the Capulet vault. The Friar, meanwhile, will inform Romeo of the plan by letter, and he and Romeo will be there when Juliet awakes. Romeo can then take her back to Mantua with him. To this desperate plan Juliet agrees.

As in III.5 where Juliet and Lady Capulet had spoken at cross purposes, so, now, there are two meanings in the exchange between Juliet and Paris.

And I am ... haste no reluctance of mine will lessen his haste

Uneven irregular, contrary to normal practice

counts accounts, considers

minded ... alone remembered or dwelt upon when she is alone

abused spoilt, marred

For it was for my face was

to my face directly, and, about my face

not mine own because, although Paris does not know this, it is Romeo's

entreat ... alone ask you to leave us alone at this time

shield forbid

compass limit

prorogue delay, postpone

presently immediately

label seal, that is, confirm another marriage by holding another hand

deed legal document, that is, a binding marriage certificate

this shall slay this knife shall slay

extremes desperate situation

commission authority

Hold wait

chide away ... shame drive away this disgrace

copest with encounters

'scape from it that is, escape from shame

charnel house small building next to a church in which were placed bones disturbed when new graves were dug

reeky shanks damp and stinking shin-bones

chapless jawless

unstained faithful, not stained with infidelity

vial small bottle

distilling liquor drink which will spread through the body

humour feeling

native progress natural movement

surcease stop

wanny wan, pale

supple government ability to move

against ... awake in preparation for your awakening

inconstant toy whim

prosperous successful

SCENE 2   Following the Friar's plan, Juliet agrees to marry Paris

Time: 'near night' on Tuesday (IV.2.39)

In the Capulet house preparations are going forward for the wedding. Juliet, falling in with the Friar's plan, submits entirely to her father, who is so pleased that he brings forward the wedding to the next day, Wednesday. Since the change of day will mean still less time for preparation, Capulet will himself stay up all night to help to get things ready in time. The scene ends on an ironic note: Capulet's heart is 'wondrous light' now that Juliet has agreed to marry Paris: the audience knows she has quite other intentions.

Act IV Scene 1 could only have taken place on Tuesday morning as both Paris and Juliet visit the Friar directly after their conversation in III.4 and III.5 at dawn on Tuesday. In this scene Juliet returns straight from that visit, so it cannot yet be, as Capulet says, 'late' on Tuesday. The time-scale is shortened for dramatic effect so that we come quickly to the crucial Tuesday night.

It is a cruel irony that Juliet's pretended change of heart is thus so effective that it contributes to the tragedy, for that lost day will help prevent Romeo learning the truth about the Friar's plan.

cunning skilful
try test
can lick their fingers proverbially the mark of a good cook
unfurnished unprepared in not having the necessary food ready
harlotry waywardness
gadding wandering
behests commands
enjoined directed
becomèd proper
closet private room
stir about busy myself

SCENE 3   **Juliet takes the Friar's potion**

Time: Tuesday night (IV.3.12–3)

Juliet sends away the Nurse (as the Friar had directed, IV.1.92) and takes the potion. As the marriage is now on Wednesday, not Thursday, she is taking it a day earlier than the Friar had planned (IV.1.89–94).

> Juliet's **soliloquy**, dwelling on her fear of the vault, enlarges what she had already said to the Friar (IV.1.80–8) and darkens the atmosphere of death which is gathering in the play. By referring us yet again to the Capulet vault, the speech reinforces the fear that in some way it is connected with the tragic climax of the play.

attires clothes
cross perverse
culled selected
behoveful needed
state ceremony
ministered provided
tried proved
strangled suffocated
like likely
conceit imagining
distraught mad
Environèd surrounded
rage madness
spit pierce through, impale

SCENE 4   Lord Capulet prepares for the wedding of Juliet and
           Paris

Time: 3 a.m. on Wednesday (IV.4.3–4)

Capulet has been up all night helping to prepare the wedding feast. These preparations generate excitement and fun, with Capulet goodnaturedly joking with the servants and ordering them about, hurrying everyone as much as he can.

This short scene gives the impression of time passing: it fills in the night while Juliet is drugged, for, at the end of the scene, we are told that the bridegroom, Paris, has arrived. Thus, it bridges Tuesday night (IV.3) and Wednesday morning (IV.5). More important, however, is its dramatically effective change of mood. Its happy and boisterous confusion is in studied contrast to the sombre quiet of Juliet's soliloquy in IV.3 and the outbursts of grief which are to follow in IV.5. The contrast sharpens our awareness that, apart from this noisy preparation and excited anticipation of the wedding, alone in her room, Juliet has taken the potion which will bring all this furious activity to nothing. In much the same way, Capulet's plans to marry Juliet to Paris in III.4 had been rendered **ironic** by our knowledge that, even as he spoke, Juliet was either with, or waiting for, Romeo in her room. In each case the audience has a fuller knowledge of the situation than have the characters on the stage and, because of this, it knows that what the characters are doing will come to nothing. In III.4 it knew, and Capulet did not, that Juliet was already married; here, it knows, and Capulet does not, that Juliet will go to the vault as if dead and not to her wedding with Paris.

pastry part of the kitchen

curfew bell bell that tolls the hour

cot-quean man who does woman's work (as Capulet had promised he would, IV.2.43)

watching staying awake, lack of sleep

whit bit

mouse hunt up at night after a woman ('mouse')

watch ... watching now watch you to make sure you don't go off at night like that now

jealous hood   jealous woman
have a head that will   have brains enough to
Mass   a common exclamation, from 'By the Mass'
whoreson   rascally fellow
loggerhead   blockhead, a pun on 'logs' in lines 16 and 18
Good Father   an exclamation, perhaps a misprint for the common 'Good Faith'
trim   dress

SCENE 5   **Juliet is discovered apparently dead**

Time: early Wednesday morning, straight after IV.5 (IV.4.25–8; IV.5.1)

The Nurse (who for the first time is not in Juliet's confidence) goes to wake Juliet and finds her apparently dead. The Friar arrives and, amidst the family's exclamations of grief, takes charge to ensure that Juliet is carried to the family vault as he had planned.

The scene is constructed to inhibit the audience from sharing the sorrow of the household, for the real cause of grief is yet to come with the true death of Juliet. The exaggerated language of the laments of the Nurse, Paris and Capulet, which almost become ridiculous; the Friar's speeches, which remind the audience that this is all part of a plan; and the comedy of the musicians with which the scene ends, all prevent the audience's sympathies from being too deeply aroused.

Fast   fast asleep
pennyworths   allowances of sleep
set up his rest   to stake all one's money at the card game of primero, and so the meaning here is 'is determined'; the Nurse means that Paris will keep Juliet awake the next night by making love to her
settled   congealed
deflowerèd by him   lost her virginity to him (that is, death)
lasting   endless, everlasting
spited   treated spitefully
Uncomfortable   depriving us of our comfort
confusion   calamity, disaster
confusions   disorders
Your part   that is, her body
his part   that is, her soul

Yet ... merriment reason, which knows there is no real cause for grief, laughs at the tears which natural affection makes us shed

put ... pipes pack up our instruments

case situation

case container for a musical instrument

'Heart's ease' a popular song of the time

'My heart is full' another song

dump a dismal tune (Peter is muddling his terms)

give it you soundly play it loudly and pay you back for refusing

gleek mockery, scorn

give you the minstrel call you a good-for-nothing

serving-creature like 'minstrel' a term of derision

pate head

carry no crotchets tolerate none of your whims; literally, 'crotchets' are musical notes

re ... fa musical notes

note understand or pay attention, a pun on 'note' meaning 'set to music'

put out display

'When griping ... silver sound' the beginning of a published poem in praise of music

griping agonising

dumps depression

Catling a lute string, and so a humorous surname for a musician

Rebeck a fiddle

Soundpost part of a violin

cry you mercy beg your pardon

for sounding for making music

ACT V

SCENE 1   Romeo, incorrectly informed that Juliet is dead, buys poison
           to kill himself in the vault where she lies

Time: later on Wednesday

The Friar's plan of feigning Juliet's death, successfully carried out in IV.5, was intended to solve the lovers' problems. In this, the very next scene, we learn that Fate is not to be so easily thwarted. Romeo, who left Juliet early on Tuesday morning in II.5, is now in Mantua. As the scene opens, he is confidently expecting good news from Verona. These hopes are dashed immediately his servant, Balthasar, arrives to tell him Juliet is dead. Although the Friar had arranged to send news to Romeo in his exile through Friar John (III.3.169–71), Romeo has heard nothing. Nor does Balthasar have any letters from the Friar for Romeo and clearly does not know the truth about Juliet's 'death'. Romeo resolves to return to Verona that night, to poison himself at the vault where Juliet lies. He buys a poison for his purpose from an apothecary in Mantua.

It is not clear from the scene itself on which day it occurs. We do know that the last scene of the play is set during the night that follows the day of this scene. Romeo is here in Mantua, and says that he will be back in Verona to lie with Juliet 'tonight' (V.1.26, 34), and in V.3 we see him arrive at the vault. But is this scene set on Wednesday, the day of Juliet's entombment (IV.5), or on Thursday? In other words, does Romeo kill himself on the night following Juliet's supposed 'death' or twenty-four hours later?

On the one hand, the Friar had said that Juliet would be drugged for forty-two hours (IV.1.105). As she took the potion on Tuesday night (IV.3), she would wake up on Thursday night. For Romeo to be there when she wakes in V.3 his 'tonight' should mean Thursday night, which would place this scene on Thursday. Later in the play, just after Juliet has woken, the Watch says she has been in the vault for two days (V.3.176), so V.3, set when it is dark, just before dawn, seems to occur very early on Friday (so that Juliet has been in the tomb on Wednesday and Thursday, two days). This again points to this scene being set on Thursday.

On the other hand, however, we learn that Balthasar left Verona immediately after seeing Juliet laid in the vault on Wednesday morning (V.1.20–1) and as Romeo intends to be back in Verona 'tonight' the journey between Mantua and Verona does not, according to Shakespeare, take long. Hence, Balthasar could arrive in Mantua on Wednesday, the day he seems to have left Verona. Another piece of evidence also suggests Wednesday for this scene.

V.3 begins with Paris performing funeral rites at Juliet's tomb, rites he says he will perform every night hereafter (V.3.16–17). It would be natural, therefore, to suppose this is the first time he has done this, which would mean this is the first night Juliet has been in the vault, namely Wednesday. He would hardly promise to perform these rites every night on the second night he visited her tomb. And this, again, would point to our scene here as on Wednesday, since Romeo meets Paris at the Capulet vault.

In the theatre, no-one is likely to remember the Friar's forty-two hours, or notice the Watch's reference to two days. The sequence of events is clear, and the impression is of a short passage of time. Watching the play, it would seem that this scene follows immediately after IV.5, that is, that it is still Wednesday. Balthasar's comment on the haste with which he has come to Romeo (V.1.21) would reinforce this impression.

If I may ... sleep if I may believe the truth of dreams which in my sleep flatter my hopes by telling me what I wish to hear

presage portend, foretell

bosom's lord i.e. heart

how sweet ... in joy when dreams of love are so full of joy, how sweet love must be in reality

presently immediately

took post post horses were swift horses available for hire at regular intervals on main roads, and so the phrase means 'to set out quickly by horse': by the same method Romeo will return to Verona (lines 26 and 33)

import suggest, signify

misadventure tragically ill-advised undertaking

see for look for

'a he

noted noticed

weeds drab clothes

Culling ... simple picking plants from which to make medicines

account collection, number

bladders used to contain liquid

packthread strong thread or twine

old ... roses rose petals pressed into small tablets

Whose sale ... death for the sale of which the penalty is immediate death
caitiff wretch miserable or wretched creature
ducats gold coins, each worth nearly ten shillings in Elizabethan money, so Romeo is offering nearly £20, a large sum
soon-speeding gear quick-acting stuff
any he any man
utters sells
starveth in thy eyes appear in your starving face
dispatch kill
cordial restorative drink (as it will restore him to Juliet)

SCENE 2 **Romeo's failure to learn the truth of the Friar's plan is explained**

Time: Wednesday

Friar John explains to Friar Laurence that he has not been able to deliver to Romeo the letter explaining Friar Laurence's plan (IV.1.113–5) because he was shut up by health officers in a house in Verona which was thought to be plague-ridden. Friar Laurence must now go to the vault alone (he, of course, does not know that Romeo has also determined to go there).

This scene confirms that Romeo will not find out the truth about Juliet's 'death'. Quickly and simply things have gone terribly wrong since IV.5.

bare-foot brother friar
associate accompany; friars usually worked in pairs
searchers men who searched out the plague by checking dead bodies
infectious pestilence plague
reign ruled, that is, the inhabitants of the house were infected
Sealed up the doors confining infected people to their homes in this way this was common practice, to prevent the spread of plague
brotherhood religious order
nice trivial
charge serious matter
dear import great importance
danger damage, harm
crow crow-bar

beshrew blame

accidents doings, events, that is, Juliet's proposed marriage to Paris and the Friar's plan to prevent it

SCENE 3 Paris, grieving at Juliet's tomb, is killed in a fight with Romeo, who then enters the vault and poisons himself. When she awakes, Juliet, seeing the body of Romeo, stabs herself. The Friar explains these events to the appalled Montagues and Capulets, who are reconciled

Time: Wednesday night to near dawn on Thursday (V.3.188–9, 305–6)

The tragic catastrophe is presented in the play's final and longest scene, a scene remarkable for its variety of dramatic mood. It begins with Paris coming to grieve at Juliet's tomb. His funeral rites establish a suitably sombre mood. But Paris is disturbed by Romeo, who has arrived from Mantua to poison himself at the vault. As Romeo begins to open the tomb, Paris steps forward to stop him. Paris believes that grief for Tybalt's death, which Romeo caused, killed Juliet, and that Romeo, as a Montague, has now come to mutilate the dead bodies of the Capulets Tybalt and Juliet. Appalled by this, he attempts to arrest Romeo. In the ensuing fight, Paris is killed. This is the first time Juliet's two lovers have met on stage, and it is only after killing him that Romeo recognises Paris.

After this sudden violence, the mood changes again as Romeo opens the vault and, in a long **soliloquy**, meditates on Juliet's beauty and prepares himself for death. Just as Romeo has drunk the poison, the Friar arrives, and, finding the bodies of Paris and Romeo, he tells the waking Juliet to fly from the place. When she realises Romeo is dead, Juliet refuses to leave and stabs herself. The Watch has been summoned by Paris's servant, and there is considerable confusion as the Capulets, Montagues and the Prince are summoned and all wonder at how these three deaths can have occurred. The Friar explains what has happened, and the scene ends as Capulet and Montague are reconciled in their grief.

The play had opened with a scene which brought to the stage the Capulets, Montagues and the Prince; its turning point in III.1 had again assembled these characters, and now, at the end, all are brought together once more. But whereas in I.1 and III.1 it was the continuance of their feud which had brought them together, now it is the ending of that feud and their reconciliation through the tragic deaths of their heirs, deaths for which, as the Prince himself says as the scene draws to a close, they and their hatred were responsible.

aloof apart

all along at full length

loose that is, the earth is loose

adventure dare

Sweet flower that is, Juliet

sweet perfumed

wanting lacking

cross interfere with

Muffle hide, conceal

letter this Romeo had written before leaving Mantua (V.1.25)

course course of action

jealous inquisitive, suspicious

hungry because Death is never satisfied

empty and therefore hungry and savage

For all this same all the same

I fear give me reason to be afraid of what he will do

maw stomach

womb belly

in despite to spite you (by forcing more 'food' in when the 'maw' is already 'gorged')

apprehend arrest

unhallowed evil

thou must die the punishment for returning from banishment

these gone these buried in the vault

For I come ... myself that is, with the poison to commit suicide

conjuration literally, casting of a magic spell; Paris means that he defies Romeo's attempt to put him off by solemn words

betossèd tossed hither and thither (by Fortune)

triumphant glorious

lantern windowed upper part of a building which admits light; to Romeo the vault is a lantern because it is lit by Juliet's beauty (lines 85–6)

feasting presence festival presence chamber, that is, the room in which a monarch would receive guests and visitors

keepers jailers

A lightning before death a proverbial phrase, describing a sudden burst of vigour just before death

ensign flag, banner

sheet winding sheet in which corpses are wrapped

To sunder ... enemy to separate from his youth him who was your enemy, that is, kill myself

And shake... flesh free this body, tired of the world, from the influence of hostile stars

dateless endless, eternal

conduct conductor, that is, the poison, which Romeo here addresses

desperate pilot that is, himself

true Apothecary the Apothecary spoke the truth (in V.1.77–9)

stumbled at stumble over. There was a superstition that to stumble was a sign that what one was doing would not turn out well

Bliss the eternal bliss of salvation in heaven

vainly in vain

unthrifty unlucky

dreamt Balthasar would actually have seen this happen: perhaps he does not want to believe that what he saw is true; perhaps (remembering it is night in a graveyard) he really does think it was a dream or hallucination; or again, perhaps he is afraid to say openly that such an awful thing has happened

masterless abandoned (by their masters or owners)

discoloured stained (with blood)

unkind unnatural

comfortable comforting

contagion contagious disease, foul influence

cup Romeo had evidently poured the poison into a cup to drink it (the apothecary had said that the poison should be taken as a drink, V.1.77–8)

timeless both 'untimely' and 'endless'

churl a mean person, here used as an affectionate rebuke

restorative that is, her kiss, which will restore her to Romeo in death

attach arrest

ground cause, explanation

without without knowing the

comes comes about

house that is, sheath

warns tolls, summons

untaught ill-mannered, used here affectionately and in sad jest

press before hurry ahead of; it was bad manners to enter a room in front of a parent

spring source of a stream, and so, cause; the **metaphor** is carried on in 'head', the beginning of a stream, and 'descent'

general leader

And let ... patience and let patience rule us in our response to misfortune

greatest that is, the one most suspect

direful dreadful, awful

both to ... excused both to accuse myself and to defend myself; the Friar knows he is guilty (his scheme caused these deaths) and yet he is innocent (that was never his intention)

date of breath span or time of breath, that is, life

stolen secret

You the Friar addresses the Capulets

perforce by force

form appearance

as on

closely secretly

privy accessory, in the secret

his its

We still ... holy man despite what you have just said, we have always known you are a holy man

post great haste

made your master was your master doing

make good confirm

therewithal with that

joys children

brace of kinsmen Mercutio and Paris were both related to the Prince

jointure marriage settlement given by the groom's family to the bride (the opposite of a dowry): Capulet means that Montague's handshake is all he can ask for as a settlement for Juliet

rate high value

Romeo's that is, Romeo's statue

lie Montague is thinking of the figures carved lying on tombs

glooming dark, sad

PART THREE

CRITICAL APPROACHES

SHAKESPEARE'S USE OF SOURCES

Nowadays it is generally assumed that a writer should invent all his or her own work and that, once a book has been published, its text belongs to the author; no-one may copy or rework it, or lift passages from it, without permission. So it comes as something of a surprise to find that in Shakespeare's time, and for hundreds of years earlier, adapting another author's work was so far from being frowned upon that it was the usual method of composition. What was valued as original was not the invention of a new story but the inventive reworking of an old one. Hence, throughout the Middle Ages and Renaissance, stories were repeated, enlarged and embellished as they were treated again and again by writers from many countries. From the modern perspective, it appears that writers from all over Europe collaborated together over many centuries.

Romeo and Juliet exemplifies this. Shakespeare, like his contemporary dramatists, seldom invented the plots of his plays. He usually borrowed them from older poems, plays or stories, and *Romeo and Juliet* is no exception. The story had already been borrowed several times before it came to Shakespeare's turn. It was first written in Italian by Masuccio Salernitano in 1476, and was then rewritten several times by Italian and French authors during the next hundred years. In 1562 the English poet Arthur Brooke, who had read it in French and Italian, published a long poem called *The Tragicall Historye of Romeus and Juliet*. This was the main source for Shakespeare's play, but Shakespeare also knew, and used, a later English prose version of the story by William Painter. Painter included 'The goodly History of the true and constant love between Rhomeo and Julietta' in a collection of tales he published in 1567 called *Palace of Pleasure*. There was also an English play on this subject, which Brooke mentions in the preface to his poem. Shakespeare may very well have seen it, may even, indeed, have had a copy of it by him as he worked on his own play. If so, what he owed to it cannot be determined, as no such play has survived. His debt to Brooke's poem, however, is considerable.

This is not to say that Shakespeare was a plagiarist. The medieval and Renaissance notion of invention is to be distinguished from simple copying. Authors were expected to reshape the sources they worked with so that the result was a text new and original in its manner and its effect. Just so, Shakespeare radically changed the emphasis and structure of the story as told by Brooke.

In Brooke's poem the story lasts nine months; in Shakespeare's play it is compressed into a few days. This stresses the remarkable suddenness of the lovers' passion. It has no time to develop: it completely overwhelms Romeo and Juliet the moment they see each other. The compression of time also highlights the fragility of their love: it is no sooner experienced than it is destroyed. After their first meeting and marriage the next day, they do not have a moment of undisturbed happiness. Troubles beset them from the start and, instead of being spread over several months, they come one upon the heels of the next with no relief and no escape. Because events happen so quickly, we have a sense that the lovers are trapped, that their final deaths are inevitable (see Plot and Structure, on Time in the Play) and, to make the time-scale clear, the timing of each scene has been given at the beginning of each scene summary.

Only in Shakespeare's play does Paris come to Juliet's tomb. This implies in him a true affection for Juliet, but, more significantly, it enables Shakespeare to achieve a dramatically effective final scene in which Juliet's two suitors confront each other at the climax of the play. Paris has been in the background throughout the play and has, unknowingly, contributed much to the unhappiness of Juliet. Here, he too is suddenly caught up by events and destroyed by them, an unsuspecting victim of the tragedy.

The character of Mercutio is entirely Shakespeare's invention. In the earlier versions of the story, Mercutio plays a very small part. (For importance as a contrast to Romeo see Characterisation.)

Shakespeare develops the characters of the Nurse and Tybalt. This extends the range of mood and attitude in the play, and achieves a dramatically effective contrast to Juliet's character in the Nurse, while Tybalt acts as a foil for Romeo and Benvolio (see Characterisation).

Shakespeare makes Juliet younger. In Brooke's poem she is sixteen, but in the play she is not yet fourteen. This increases her vulnerability, but, more important, it makes more striking her development from a young and submissive girl, who is very ready to obey her parents early in the play, to a self-reliant, defiant and tragic heroine who knows her own mind at the end. By stressing her youth Shakespeare stresses this contrast between Juliet's character before and after she has met Romeo. He makes her early obedience to her parents the more credible and her later resolution to defy them the more remarkable. (For Juliet's development see Love of Romeo and Juliet.)

Shakespeare's poetry is a more subtle and affective (i.e. emotional) medium. This is an obvious remark, but the consequence is that in every scene the effects are more varied and more moving than in the source. To read *Romeo and Juliet* is an entirely different – and much richer – experience than reading Brooke's poem.

PLOT AND STRUCTURE: REALISM AND ROMANCE

SINGLE PLOT

Romeo and Juliet is firmly centred on the figures of its hero and heroine: one or other of them is nearly always on stage. There is no sub-plot, no secondary story, such as Shakespeare and other Elizabethan dramatists often introduced into their plays. It is the story of Romeo and Juliet that holds our attention throughout; the play's straightforward plot charts the course of their love. In Act I they meet; in Act II they declare their love and are secretly married; in Acts III and IV they try to overcome the obstacles in the way of their relationship, but these efforts are tragically frustrated in Act V. There is thus a clear structure: an optimistic and often comic movement up to the marriage at the end of Act II is followed by a counter-movement, which begins with the quarrel in III.1 and leads to tragedy. This clear design means that there is something relentless about the progress of the play: despite variations in mood and pace, there is no extended digression or relief from the tragic tale.

TIME IN THE PLAY

This is emphasised by the time-scale of the play. Compressing events into a few days was one of Shakespeare's most significant changes to the story as it occurred in his source (see Shakespeare's Use of Sources). As a result, the action of the play lasts only four days. From Capulet's question 'What day is this?', to which Paris replies 'Monday, my lord' (III.4.18–19), the day on which each scene occurs can be determined. What matters in the theatre, though, is not the actual day but the short time sequence. That Romeo and Juliet marry only the day after they first met is the point, not that they meet on a Sunday and marry on a Monday. Nevertheless, the names of the days are a convenient help when summarising the sequence of events, and they are used in what follows:

Act I opens at 9 a.m. on Sunday morning (I.1.161) and culminates in Capulet's party on Sunday evening. Act II takes us through Sunday night to dawn on Monday (II.2.176; II.3.1–2) and to the marriage of the lovers in II.6 on Monday afternoon (II.4.176–9). The quarrel that opens Act III is later on Monday afternoon (III.1.112–13), and by III.4.34–5 it is late that night. Romeo leaves Juliet in III.5 as the dawn breaks on Tuesday, and Juliet's marriage to Paris, originally planned for Thursday (III.4.17–21) is brought forward to the next day, Wednesday (IV.2.23–37). Early on Wednesday morning Juliet is discovered apparently dead (IV.5.3–4). Later that day Romeo learns, as he thinks, of Juliet's death, and that night kills himself at her tomb. The play ends as dawn is about to break on Thursday (V.3.188–9, 305–6). The play thus lasts from Sunday morning until the night of the following Wednesday/Thursday.

Such a short and consistent time-scale (even allowing for the slight difficulty about V.1 – see Summary Act V) is very rare in Elizabethan drama. By keeping the sequence of events clearly before the audience Shakespeare makes the tragedy the more pitiful simply because of the swiftness with which events occur. The action seems to rush on at headlong speed. 'I stand on sudden haste' says Romeo (II.3.89), and he does seem to be engaged in a race against time. Everything in the play happens at great speed. The lovers hurry into marriage, and Romeo is immediately hurried into banishment. The moment Romeo hears of Juliet's death he posts back to Verona to kill himself. In all this haste, the love of Romeo and Juliet is very short-lived. Of Romeo's avowal of love Juliet says:

> ... Although I joy in thee,
> I have no joy of this contract tonight.
> It is too rash, too unadvised, too sudden;
> Too like the lightning, which doth cease to be
> Ere one can say 'It lightens'. (II.2.116–20)

Lightning is but momentary. As Romeo prepares to kill himself he uses the word again:

> How oft when men are at the point of death
> Have they been merry! which their keepers call
> A lightning before death. O how may I
> Call this a lightning? (V.3.88–91)

Because of the time-scale of the play the love of Romeo and Juliet does seem to be a 'lightning before death'. It has no sooner come to them than it is taken from them.

COINCIDENCES AND IMPROBABILITIES IN THE ACTION

The main line of the action may be clear and the structure of the play simple, but to set down the story in bald prose may well make it sound incredible. Even if it is allowed that two young people could fall so completely in love so suddenly as do Romeo and Juliet, is it credible that they would change so completely to do so? When the play opens, Romeo is infatuated with Rosaline to an extraordinary degree. His melancholy behaviour because she rejects him is the first thing the audience learns about him (I.1.116–238) and his anguished passion is the butt of Mercutio's jokes in I.4 and II.1. For her part, Juliet, when we first meet her, has no thoughts of love or marriage, and is fully prepared to follow her parents' wishes in looking favourably on Paris (I.3.67, 98–100). And yet, in a moment, Romeo forgets Rosaline (I.5.44–53) and Juliet is thinking of marriage to an enemy (I.5.134–5). Still more improbable is the elaborate plan of Friar Laurence, involving a potion which is almost magical in its effect.

On top of these central elements in the plot there is an extraordinary number of coincidences in the play, all unfortunate. That Romeo should fall in love with the daughter of an enemy house is the central, tragic, chance event. That Paris should come as suitor to Juliet at just this time is another coincidence which hastens the tragedy. That Friar Laurence's letter should not be delivered is another; that Romeo should kill himself *just before* Juliet awakes is another; that the Friar should arrive at the vault *just after* Romeo has taken poison, another. Had any of these chances fallen out differently there would have been no tragedy. Romeo, for example, would have found Juliet awake had he come a little later or she woken a little earlier. Thinking of cases like this, it is hard not to feel that Romeo and Juliet are killed by cruel chance, or fate. If Romeo's luck had been different, Friar John would have come sooner and told him the truth about Juliet's 'death'. But Romeo has no luck in this play. He and Juliet are the victims of an extraordinary succession (even an incredible succession) of mischances (see also Tragedy, on Fate).

There are other odd things about the action of the play. How can Lady Capulet know that Romeo is living in Mantua before he can possibly have arrived there and when his destination is anyway a secret (III.5.88)? When Juliet is discovered apparently dead in IV.5, why does no-one wonder why she died? No-one suspects suicide or foul play, and no-one notices the vial that must lie beside her (IV.3.20, 23). Why is it that the Friar, who expected Juliet to awake after forty-two hours (IV.1.104–5), arrives late at the vault on a matter of such urgency? How can Romeo, who has only just arrived in Mantua, have already discovered, and remembered, an apothecary's shop where he can buy poison? He had no idea he would ever need it, after all, and yet in V.1 it is immediately in his mind. Or again, why are Montagues and Capulets at each other's throats? What is the cause of their quarrel? We are never told. One last example: if we are to believe this feud stands in the way of Romeo's love for Juliet, what do we make of the fact that it did not stand in the way of his love for Rosaline? Rosaline was also a Capulet (I.2.68, 81–2), and yet Romeo had been able to see her because we know she refused him. If he could see her, why not Juliet?

Clearly, this is not a realistic text. Realism is a comparatively recent literary convention, established by the novel in the eighteenth and nineteenth centuries. Earlier literature did not attempt to depict everyday life, and therefore did not value either consistency or authenticity in its details. Hence, although *Romeo and Juliet* is set in Italy, there is no attempt to represent Italian customs accurately. Capulet's household is a typical English Elizabethan household; the masked dance at Capulet's party was fashionable in Elizabethan England and the description of the apothecary's shop (V.1.40–8) would have fitted many such shops in Elizabethan London. All through the play, proverbs, idioms and exclamations are thoroughly English. Indeed, at one point Mercutio makes fun of the Italian style of duelling which had recently become fashionable in England (II.4.19–26). This might be expected from an Englishman and it would go down well with an English audience; to object that Mercutio is supposed to be Italian, and so would never say such a thing, is beside the point. The play will not offer that kind of **verisimilitude** (likeness to reality).

THE PATTERN OF THE ACTION

Romeo and Juliet, then, does not tell a story that is correct and accurate in all its circumstantial details, believable in all its incidents. There is a story running through the whole play, and in a general way it holds together, but the kind of questions posed a moment ago cannot be answered because Shakespeare gives no answers. The reason is that the story as such is the least important part of the play. The plot is only the starting-point, the means by which characters are brought together for striking confrontations and in dramatically varied scenes. How they get there does not interest Shakespeare nearly so much as the scenes themselves. The very characters themselves are chosen not as 'real' human beings, but to contrast and complement each other in effective ways (see Characterisation). However we may quibble about the story of the lovers, when Romeo and Juliet speak to each other in II.2 there is no doubting the persuasiveness of their love. It is for such moments as that expression of genuine love that the plot exists.

What structures the play is, hence, not a plausible plot but a succession of complementary and contrasting incidents and scenes (such as are noticed in the scene summaries). *Romeo and Juliet* is a tragedy, but it is also, in performance, a play of remarkably varied moods and actions, all carefully contrived. The very first scene illustrates how the whole play works. It begins with comedy from the servants, but the mood quickly changes and there is a fight and a riot, with citizens pouring onto the stage shouting and fighting. This uproar is suddenly silenced by the appearance of the Prince who, in another change of mood, delivers an impressive and threatening long speech to his subjects. The stage then clears for new matter in a different tone. It is a family discussion about the peculiar behaviour of Romeo. When he comes on, the scene ends as it had begun, with only two people talking, but now it is not the bawdy talk of the servants we hear but the sophisticated language of love. In only just over 200 lines, Shakespeare has provided merriment, spectacle and unease; and he has also, of course, set the scene for the play. In just this way the audience's interest is maintained throughout the play. The quiet scene, II.6, is followed by the violence of III.1; Juliet's **soliloquy** in IV.3 contrasts with the bustle of IV.4; the comedy of the musicians which ends IV.5 contrasts with the outcries of grief earlier in that scene. Examples could be multiplied.

Such manipulation of the sequence of the action makes for a variety of mood and incident; it also makes for unpredictability: the audience is never quite sure what to expect next. Above all, it makes for the dramatic and poetic exploration of themes and situations which bear upon the audience's experience, despite the play's neglect of realism. *Romeo and Juliet* is a romantic tale of love which does not belong to the ordinary everyday world of cause and effect, but this is not to say that the play is merely romance in the sense of a fanciful piece of art irrelevant to our lives.

THEMES: LOVE AND HATE

THE LOVE OF ROMEO AND JULIET

Love has a transforming effect upon both Romeo and Juliet. At the beginning of the play, Romeo is a rather tiresome young man, endlessly complaining, in the elaborate language of love then fashionable, about his sorrows because Rosaline rejects him. He is playing the part of the Petrarchan lover. The love poetry of the medieval Italian poet Francesco **Petrarch** (1304–74) was widely imitated throughout the Renaissance. It established literary conventions of how to behave and how to talk when in love. In Elizabethan love poetry we meet, over and over again, lovers who behave just like Romeo. They dote upon one lady; live only for her; express their feelings in elaborate **conceits** and rhetorical phrases; they are devastated if she frowns on them and overwhelmed by joy if she smiles. It is an elaborate, exaggerated ideal, almost a religion of love.

Mercutio recognises the fashionable posturing of Romeo's behaviour when he says 'Now is he for the numbers that Petrarch flowed in' (II.4.38–9). So Romeo regards Rosaline as beyond all women in beauty: 'The all-seeing sun / Ne'er saw her match since first the world begun.' (I.2.91–2).

And he swears his love for her in religious terms – he worships her, and resorts to ingenious imagery to say so (for example I.2.87–90). He talks of his depression at her rejection of him in the same exaggerated way. It is difficult not to feel that he is wallowing in self-pity (for example I.1.186–94), and the **oxymorons** (combinations of words of opposite meanings) with which he endeavours to describe his feelings sound very much like contrivance:

> Why then, O brawling love, O loving hate,
> O anything, of nothing first create!
> O heavy lightness, serious vanity,
> Misshapen chaos of well-seeming forms,
> Feather of lead, bright smoke, cold fire, sick health,
> Still-waking sleep, that is not what it is! (1.1.176–81)

There is much to be said for the idea that Romeo is in love with the idea of being in love, and an audience is likely to have a good deal of sympathy with Benvolio's attempts to make Romeo see sense and Mercutio's efforts to mock him from his moanings. On stage the sight of neither of Romeo's two friends taking his 'love' too seriously would strengthen and audience's suspicions that this is a very young man playing love games.

When Romeo sees Juliet, the character of his extravagant avowals changes. The speech in which he first sees her has a new tenderness and awe in it:

> O, she doth teach the torches to burn bright!
> It seems she hangs upon the cheek of night
> As a rich jewel in an Ethiop's ear -
> Beauty too rich for use, for earth too dear!
> So shows a snowy dove trooping with crows
> As yonder lady o'er her fellows shows …
> Did my heart love till now? Forswear it, sight!
> For I ne'er saw true beauty till this night. (I.5.44–53)

That last line is a confession that all he said before was wrongheaded. **Ironically**, Benvolio had told Romeo that if he went to Capulet's party and saw Rosaline in the company of other ladies, he would realise she was not at all exceptional (I.2.93–8). Rosaline is indeed displaced, but by a deeper affection than Benvolio ever expected. The Friar is later amazed at Romeo's fickleness (II.3.61–76), but this is not the simple fickleness of a man exchanging one shallow love for another. It is a change from a shallow affection to a binding love. Although Romeo is always prone to lapse again into extravagant language, there is no doubting the new depth of his feelings. He is, after all, constant to Juliet to death. Shakespeare stresses this change by making Rosaline only a name. We cannot take too seriously protestations of love for a woman we never see or hear.

Juliet is never posturingly foolish in the way of Romeo but she, too, undergoes a change. At the beginning of the play she is modest, subdued and quiet. When her mother suggests that Paris might make a good husband, she simply replies:

> I'll look to like, if looking liking move.
>
> But no more deep will I endart mine eye
>
> Than your consent gives strength to make it fly. (I.3.98–100)

She is prepared to be guided entirely by her parents. For Juliet, the meeting with Romeo is an awakening to the fact that love is more than filial obedience, and with this she discovers a new resolution. She flatly contradicts her promise of obedience by marrying Romeo secretly. And she emerges as a strong and practical personality – far more so than Romeo. In the balcony scene, she addresses Romeo directly and plainly, asking down-to-earth questions to which Romeo replies with elaborate images (for example II.2.62–9). When she discovers that Romeo has overheard her confessing her love for him, she does not deny it, but with startling and winning directness dismisses the conventions of courtship: 'Fain would I dwell on form – fain, fain deny / What I have spoke. But farewell compliment!' (II.2.88–9). Shakespeare admired this kind of honesty: it appears in other heroines of his (for example, Miranda in *The Tempest*, III.1.48–91). And it is Juliet, we notice, who first mentions marriage, and sets Romeo on to arrange it (II.2.143–8). (For Juliet's plain language, see The Language of Love.) No less than Romeo's, her commitment is absolute and unconditional, quite heedless of social convention and family ties.

COMPETING VIEWS OF LOVE

The love of Romeo and Juliet is at odds with the world in which they find themselves, but the play does not straightforwardly oppose admirable lovers and detestable inhabitants of Verona. The other characters in the play are not without sympathetic qualities, nor are their views deprived of cogency. On the contrary, it is through these characters, none of whom can simply be dismissed, that the love of Romeo and Juliet is interrogated.

Juliet's father, Capulet, is a case in point. Were he simply overbearing and tyrannical, Juliet's disobedience could be applauded. He is certainly very cruel to Juliet in III.5, but that is not all there is to him. He is so angry then because he is bitterly disappointed. We know he has great affection for his daughter and hopes she will have a happy future (I.2.7–19). He believes she grieves for the death of her cousin Tybalt, and thinks that marriage to Paris will make her happy. This is why he agrees to the marriage without consulting her (III.4.12–28), as Juliet's mother says and Paris later explains to the Friar (III.5.107–10; IV.1.6–15). He is angry when Juliet refuses in III.5 because his plans for her happiness are frustrated. Capulet is not simply a cruel father, a tyrant over his daughter. The audience is consequently aware of what can be said on his part, and that Juliet does wrong in going against him. There is some sympathy for him both when he thinks Juliet is dead (IV.5) and when she really is so (V.3).

It is not, then, the case that Shakespeare surrounds two ideal lovers with unfeeling and unpleasant people, who alienate the audience. The lovers are not simply set in opposition to wrongheaded and malevolent friends and relatives. Rather, they are set among well-intentioned people who each have their own ideas on the nature of love. As a result, the love of Romeo and Juliet is only one among several kinds of love articulated in the play. *Romeo and Juliet* is a play about two young lovers in conflict with their parents and families, but it is also a play about competing ideas of love.

ROMANTIC AND UNROMANTIC LOVE

Among these are romantic and unromantic ideas of love. Romeo and Juliet are romantic. They give their all and disregard everything else. For Capulet, however, love and marriage are matters to be decided by a prudent father with the best interests of his daughter at heart. For Lady Capulet, Juliet's mother, they seem to be matters of worldly wisdom. She is a rather curt, sharp woman. She is only about twenty-eight years old (in I.3.72–4 she says she was a mother at about Juliet's age, and Juliet is now nearly fourteen), yet her husband is an old man (I.1.90; I.2.3; I.5.22–5), well past the age for dancing (I.5.31–41). To him, Lady Capulet speaks abruptly, often reminding him of his age (for example I.1.76). She seems to have little love for him in the romantic sense (for example IV.4.11–12) and the difference in their ages leads to the suspicion that it was an arranged marriage – a sensible move in order to achieve a good position in the world. Like Capulet himself, she has no patience with Juliet's refusal of her father's prudent scheme (III.5.203–4). Because of their views on love, neither parent can understand why Juliet should possibly want to decline such a handsome offer of marriage as is proposed with Paris.

In a different way, Benvolio is also sensible in his approach to love. In the early scenes of the play he tries to show Romeo that his affection for Rosaline is extravagant and unwarranted. He points out that if Romeo were to see her with other women he would realise she is nothing exceptional (I.2.85–6, 93–8). He does not treat Romeo's affection quite seriously, and wonders that Romeo can go through such agonies. That Romeo's affection for Rosaline is not genuine does not affect the common sense of what Benvolio says. He would almost certainly have said the same thing about Romeo's love for Juliet, had he known of it.

SPIRITUAL AND SEXUAL LOVE

Shakespeare, then, gives us prudent, sensible, worldly wise attitudes to love, from people who have Romeo's best interests at heart. So, too, there are realistic and earthy attitudes to love in conflict with more spiritual ideals. The amount of bawdy talk – the number of jokes about and references to sex – is a striking feature of the play. This is, indeed, how it begins, with Sampson and Gregory making ribald jests about male erections and taking women's virginity. For these servants, the relation-ships between men and women are clearly a matter of sex only. Throughout the play the love of Romeo and Juliet is set in a context of such lewd talk which has no time for notions of love. The Nurse is forever making sexual puns and innuendoes. She repeats with relish her husband's joke when the baby Juliet falls down:

'A was a merry man – took up the child.
'Yea,' quoth he, 'dost thou fall upon thy face?
Thou wilt fall backward when thou hast more wit.
Wilt thou not, Jule?' (I.3.41–4)

The point of the joke is, of course, that Juliet will lie on her back when a man makes love to her. The Nurse anticipates the sexual pleasures of Juliet's wedding night with Romeo (II.5.75) and with Paris (IV.5.5–7) with the same glee. Indeed, that the Nurse can suggest that Juliet should go ahead and marry Paris even though she is already married to Romeo (III.5.213–26) shows that the Nurse has scant regard for loyalty or any of the usual virtues of love. Morality and high feeling mean little to her – she sees sex as the essential thing in the relationship between men and women. Certainly the love between Juliet and Romeo is sexually consummated (and only a day after they have first met), but it is not the insatiability of sexual desire which drives them together. Sexuality is a part, not the essence, of their relationship; it is the expression of a love which involves more than desire, and not the whole point of love, as it is for the Nurse.

Mercutio, too, has little patience with Romeo's high feelings. He has a down-to-earth remedy for Romeo: 'If love be rough with you, be rough with love' (I.4.27). He cannot see the sense of Romeo's 'dumps' and by his jokes constantly makes fun of Romeo's pretensions. He mocks Romeo's extravagant passion (II.1.6–21), and by his insinuations suggests it is all a fraud to disguise simple sexual passion (II.1.33–8). Again, the point should be made that these are the views of characters who hold Juliet and Romeo dear; they cannot simply be dismissed as malevolent or unfeeling.

PASSION AND MODERATION

Another opposition is that between passion and moderation. The Friar, who as 'ghostly father' to both Romeo and Juliet is much concerned for their spiritual welfare, often speaks against uncontrolled passion. It was, he says, that Romeo 'doted' on Rosaline, not that he 'loved' her, which he disapproved of (II.3.77–8). That is, he disapproved of unreasonable infatuation ('doting'), not what he calls 'love'. But, clearly, for the Friar love is a thing of moderation. Feelings should always be controlled. He does not like the sudden haste of the impetuous lover Romeo – 'Wisely and slow. They stumble that run fast' (II.3.90) – and is suspicious of great passion:

> These violent delights have violent ends
> And in their triumph die, like fire and powder,
> Which as they kiss consume. (II.6.9–11)

He directs Romeo to 'love moderately'. Such a love, he believes, will last (II.6.14–15).

WERE ROMEO AND JULIET WRONG?

These, then, are some of the conflicting attitudes to love in the play. The hero and heroine are surrounded not by people who, all in their different ways, advise against extreme passion and unconsidered love. Their advice makes sense, the more so when we remember that Juliet herself was half-afraid that what the lovers experience was too sudden to be sincere (II.2.116–20). And in one way, of course, everyone else in the play is right. The romantic love of Romeo and Juliet does lead to their death. It is quite true that they act without forethought, without consideration of the consequences, that they are consumed by their love, and that the result is that they die. And to an Elizabethan audience it would have been plainer than it perhaps is to modern spectators that Romeo and Juliet did wrong to marry in secret without their parents' consent. This would have been a serious act of disobedience at that time. Indeed, Arthur Brooke had seen this as the point of the tragedy. In the preface to his poem, he explained that he believes Romeo and Juliet were justly punished for their immoderate passion and their defiance of proper authority in arranging a secret marriage. Brooke calls their love 'unhonest desire', and rebukes Romeo and Juliet for ignoring their parents and making use of 'dronken gosyppes' and 'superstitious friers' in order to satisfy their 'wished lust'. To his mind, they shamefully abused 'the honorable name of lawefull mariage' and thoroughly deserved to die for their 'unhonest lyfe'.

Is this the import of Shakespeare's play? Do Romeo and Juliet deserve the criticism they received from the other characters? Are they justly punished?

THE FEUD

The answer is, no. Shakespeare's play actually inverts Brooke's poem. His radical reworking of his source draws from it quite another meaning. On the one hand, the attractiveness of the lovers' characters and the poetic beauty of the scenes in which they meet demand that an audience responds wholly and totally to their love. On the other hand, the parents whom Romeo and Juliet defy are engaged in a feud. The love of the hero and heroine is set in a context of hate. This is an extremely significant point to grasp. The play's first scene is concerned with this feud; we are made aware of it before ever we meet Romeo or Juliet – indeed, the 'ancient grudge' between the 'two households' is the very first thing the Chorus mentions in the Prologue (lines 1–4). How this feud began is never revealed (and so we cannot take sides), but throughout the play the audience is constantly reminded of it. The 'fiery Tybalt', who appears in the first scene, is in the background throughout the early scenes of the play. His determination not to let the matter of Romeo's intrusion into Capulet's party drop (I.5.91–2) raises ominous fears about what he will do. And in III.1, the turning-point of the play, the worst comes about. The feud is directly responsible for the secret marriage, Romeo's banishment, and so for the Friar's scheme which leads to the deaths of the lovers. In short, it is hate which kills Romeo and Juliet in Shakespeare's play. It is only because they belong to enemy families that all the apprehension and secrecy are necessary. And only because of that do things go so badly wrong.

It is now clearer why the play devotes so much space to this feud: it is the feud which vindicates Romeo and Juliet in their rejection of all social and familial ties for love. Everyone else in the play may be full of good sense about love, but they are all also obsessively hostile to each other, enslaved to hatred. This fatally flaws everything they say on the subject, for it is evident that the capacity to move beyond prejudice is quite beyond them. Romeo and Juliet alone are not subject to this obsession. They alone have escaped. They want nothing to do with the feud. Romeo clearly does his very best not to become involved in III.1. Shakespeare here makes an effective alteration to the story as told in Brooke's poem. There, Romeo and Tybalt alone fight. By making Romeo refuse, only to be drawn in by the death of his friend Mercutio, Shakespeare makes it plain that Romeo was an unwilling combatant. In short, the world of Romeo and Juliet's love, in II.2 and III.5, seems a haven of peace and love, removed from all this brawling and hate.

THE TRIUMPH OF LOVE

This haven is very short-lived and cruelly destroyed. There is no escaping the senseless horror of that, but neither is that a complete account of the play's ending. The Prince tries to stop the feuding, but in vain; the Friar hopes that the marriage of Romeo and Juliet may unite the families, but his scheme goes terribly wrong. Neither the Church (the Friar) nor the State (the Prince), with all their worldly wisdom, all their common sense, can end the hatred. But the love of Romeo and Juliet can. The awful, tragic price to be paid is their deaths, but for this the responsibility lies not with them but with the Montagues and Capulets. And it is their deaths, compelling Capulet and Montague to recognise how wickedly foolish is their feud, which reconcile them. In this respect, the last 150 lines of the play, following the deaths of Romeo and Juliet, which might seem an anti-climax, are crucial. It is here that the redemptive work of the tragedy is achieved. As the Friar explains at length the tricks and deceits Romeo and Juliet had been put to by their families' hostility for each other, shame grows in Capulet and Montague, and, realising what they have done, in their grief and guilt they are reconciled.

So the play ends not with the deaths of Romeo and Juliet, but in reconciliation. It ends with the triumph of love. To the feuding world of Verona, peace and harmony are restored by the fates of Romeo and Juliet. This is only possible (and this is the point) because Romeo and Juliet did not listen to anyone's advice. It was only because they were true to each other, that they defied the world and neglected its advice, that they were killed; and it was only because of this that hatred finally died. Had the play ended with their deaths, all would have been lost; as it is, the play ends with positive gain. Had Shakespeare not dwelt on the feud, the play would have shown love destroyed and would have been an unrelievedly pessimistic play. As it is, though love is destroyed, it is not destroyed in vain. The price to be paid is very high – we may feel, too high – as it always is in tragedy, but this is not a play only about loss. Its drift is to demonstrate in love an ability to heal old wounds, of which no-one else's idea of love in the play has any understanding.

TRAGEDY: FOREBODING AND FATE

This brings us to the essential paradox of tragedy, or, at least, of Shakespearean tragedy, that, despite its appalling sadness, it holds gain and loss in an unresolved tension. Shakespeare's tragedies can be almost unbearably grim in their injustice (no-one could argue that Romeo and Juliet deserve to die), but they are not straightforwardly pessimistic, hopeless plays. *Romeo and Juliet* vindicates the lovers even as it destroys them. Their love bring about reconciliation and peace at the terrible cost of their deaths. The play generates both relief that they did not die in vain, and overwhelming sadness that they had to die at all. The two things go hand in hand: it is because Romeo and Juliet are the lovers they are that they deserve life, and yet it is precisely because they are the lovers they are that they have to die. The point can be put the other way around: were they not such lovers they would have lived, but then, their love would hardly have been remarkable and could have had no regenerating effect; the feud would have continued too. It would have been a much sadder – indeed, a hopeless – play, had Romeo and Juliet submitted and decided never to see each other again. This is the central **irony** of Shakespearean tragedy: the audience suffers because it so much wants a happy ending even it knows that this is impossible, that, in some awful way, it is better that the protagonists die.

INEVITABILITY IN THE PLAY

In *Romeo and Juliet* it is quite clear that the lovers do have to die, that they are doomed. Shakespeare's conception of tragedy in this early play depicts the lovers as the victims of circumstances. They are not responsible for their fates: a terrible succession of mischances destroys them. Had any one of so many things been different, all would have been well. Had Friar Laurence's letter been delivered … had Juliet woken earlier … and so on. These coincidences are hardly realistic (see Coincidences … in the Action), but they do serve an important dramatic purpose: the fact that things keep going against the lovers creates the impression that a hostile and malign fate is at work. This view is encouraged throughout the play.

Right at the start, the Chorus announces that we are to see a 'pair of star-crossed lovers' (line 6) and from then on there are repeated ominous suggestions that Romeo and Juliet are fated to die. Even before Romeo has seen Juliet, as he is about to join Capulet's party he says:

> … my mind misgives
> Some consequence, yet hanging in the stars,
> Shall bitterly begin his fearful date
> With this night's revels and expire the term
> Of a despised life, closed in my breast,
> By some vile forfeit of untimely death. (I.4.106–11)

He is, of course, right, and the audience, hearing these lines, fears as much. The moment after they have met, each lover has a similar foreboding that this love will end in disaster. When Benvolio says, 'Away, be gone. The sport is at the best', Romeo replies, 'Ay, so I fear', meaning he fears things can only get worse from now on (I.5.119–20). And Juliet, learning Romeo's identity from the Nurse, says 'Prodigious birth of love it is to me / That I must love a loathed enemy' (I.5.140–1). In the balcony scene, when they declare their love, Juliet mistrusts this sudden passion (II.2.116–20). Romeo goes to marry Juliet with a challenge to fate on his lips – 'Then love-devouring death do what he dare' (II.6.7) – and an Elizabethan audience would know that fate has a habit of accepting such challenges. As the lovers part, Juliet asks Romeo 'O, thinkest thou we shall ever meet again?'; Romeo tries to reassure her, but she replies:

> O God, I have an ill-divining soul!
> Methinks I see thee, now thou art so low,
> As one dead in the bottom of a tomb. (III.5.54–6)

The next time she sees Romeo he is, indeed, dead in the bottom of a tomb. Romeo's dream, which he recounts as he waits in Mantua for news from Verona, has a similarly ominous note: 'I dreamt my lady came and found me dead' (V.1.6). When Romeo hears the news of Juliet's death, he turns on fate: 'I defy you, stars' he cries (V.1.24). As he looks on the dead Paris, he thinks of the two of them as the victims of circumstances, both written 'in sour misfortune's book' (V.3.82), and, as he prepares to kill himself, he says he will 'shake the yoke of inauspicious stars / From this world-wearied flesh' (V.3.111–12). And the Friar himself, who had tried to help these 'star-crossed' lovers, admits there was nothing he could do against the fate which seems to have worked against them: 'A greater power than we can contradict / Hath thwarted our intents' (V.3.153–4).

References like these throughout the play steadily increase the air of foreboding and strengthen the impression, which the sad succession of hostile chances has given, that there is nothing Romeo and Juliet can do. They seem helpless. The curse of a dying man was, to Elizabethans, particularly ominous, and the dying Mercutio cries three times 'A plague a'both your houses' (III.1.91, 99–100, 108). The point is plain.

JULIET AS THE BRIDE OF DEATH

One recurring kind of remark works particularly strongly to darken the atmosphere of the play. Time and again Shakespeare introduces the idea that Juliet will be the bride of Death. She herself first speaks like this the moment after she has first met Romeo: 'Go ask his name. – If he be married, / My grave is like to be my wedding bed' (I.5.134–5). When she hears of Romeo's banishment she looks at the ropes which were to have brought Romeo to her room, and resolves:

> He made you for a highway to my bed,
> But I, a maid, die maiden-widowèd.
> Come, cords. Come, Nurse. I'll to my wedding bed,
> And death, not Romeo, take my maidenhead. (III.2.134–7)

Lady Capulet reminds the audience of this way of thinking about Juliet when she exclaims, in her anger at Juliet's refusal to marry Paris, 'I would the fool were married to her grave' (III.5.140), and Juliet's father, Capulet, speaks similarly when he thinks Juliet is dead:

> Death is my son-in-law. Death is my heir.
> My daughter he hath wedded. I will die
> And leave him all. Life, living, all is death's. (IV.5.38–40)

Paris, weeping at the vault, thinks that he grieves by Juliet's bridal bed (V.3.12), and finally, Romeo, preparing to join Juliet in death, and seeing her beauty, thinks Death loves her and this keeps her beautiful:

> … Ah, dear Juliet,
> Why art thou yet so fair? Shall I believe
> That unsubstantial death is amorous,
> And that the lean abhorrèd monster keeps
> Thee here in dark to be his paramour? (V.3.101–5)

Remarks like these mean that death is always in the back of the minds of the audience; they encourage us to expect it to be the result of the lovers' affair and so impress on us the hopelessness of their situation.

FATE AND CHANCE

In this play, then, Shakespeare's idea of tragedy is of a hostile fate working against the lovers. Through no fault of their own, circumstances are repeatedly arranged to work against them. This is the old medieval idea of tragedy. In his later tragedies Shakespeare made it more problematic through introducing more complex causes that involve the aspirations, choices and misconceptions of the tragic protagonists themselves. In plays like *King Lear* and *Othello*, though the tragic heroes are both the victims of hostile circumstances, they are also complicit in their tragedies in a way that is not true of Romeo and Juliet. To a degree, Lear brings his death upon himself, through his pride, his indolence, his passion, his prejudice. It is Othello's vulnerability to Iago's false suggestion that his wife, Desdemona, is unfaithful, that kills both him and her. That vulnerability is a construction of personal, social, political and sexual features far more complex than anything in *Romeo and Juliet*.

In *Romeo and Juliet*, chance is paramount. Romeo's impetuosity may contribute something to the tragedy (see Characterisation), but the marriage is not a wrong decision, whereas Othello was simply wrong to believe that Desdemona was unfaithful. It may have been an unwise decision to get married, but the price they pay far exceeds what that should incur. It is fate which determines that the lovers should be born of enemy families, that Mercutio should be killed by Tybalt, that Friar Laurence's letter should not be delivered. This is what destroys them; they are to be pitied as innocent victims.

This is certainly how Romeo and Juliet speak of themselves. After killing Tybalt Romeo exclaims 'O, I am fortune's fool' (III.1.136), and later he speaks of his 'betossed soul' (V.3.76), suggesting that, like a helpless ship in a storm, he is blown hither and thither by fate. And when she learns she must marry Paris Juliet exclaims in despair that she is the weak victim of fate's schemes: 'Alack, alack, that heaven should practise stratagems / Upon so soft a subject as myself!' (III.5.210–11). Shakespeare's presentation thus invites sympathy, and is quite unlike the moral indignation of his source, the poem by Brooke (see Themes – Were Romeo and Juliet Wrong?).

STYLE: WORDPLAY AND PLAIN SPEAKING

LINGUISTIC CHANGES

On first reading, the words on the page of a Shakespeare play, particularly one like *Romeo and Juliet*, can seem very odd indeed. This is explicable partly in terms of linguistic change during the 400 years since Shakespeare wrote; words change their senses, colloquial expressions go out of fashion, idioms alter. Often a curious-looking line in Shakespeare can be explained in this way. The very first line of *Romeo and Juliet* is an example: 'Gregory, on my word, we'll not carry coals'. Sampson and Gregory do not put a sack of coals down on the stage in disgust, nor does Sampson mean that he is not going to fetch any for Capulet. He is using a proverbial expression which has now fallen into disuse: his meaning is that he is not going to put up with any insults from the Montagues. On first appearance, Mercutio's remark to Romeo, 'Tut, dun's the mouse, the constable's own word' (I.4.40), looks very like nonsense. Again, Mercutio is using a colloquialism that has gone out of fashion. His meaning is simply 'be quiet', 'stop talking like that'.

A greater risk of misinterpretation is posed by words and phrases which look familiar enough, for the meanings of many words still in use have changed since Elizabethan times. Consequently, many lines which appear to make good sense actually carry a meaning quite contrary to the sense we take from them. When Tybalt is angry because Romeo has come to Capulet's party, Capulet tries to calm him, and says: 'Here in my house do him no disparagement. / Therefore be patient; take no note of him' (I.5.70–1). Capulet does not mean that Tybalt should be patient, ignore Romeo now, and wait for another opportunity; he means quite the opposite, that Tybalt should be calm and forget about Romeo altogether. When Juliet, in the balcony scene, says to Romeo, 'In truth, fair Montague, I am too fond' (II.2.98), a modern reader is likely to understand 'fond' to mean 'affectionate', and so suppose Juliet is saying that she likes Romeo too much. 'Fond' did have this meaning in the Elizabethan period, but it also meant 'foolish' and that meaning is not excluded here. Juliet is saying that she may seem silly in liking Romeo so much so suddenly. Unless both senses of the word 'fond' are recognised, only half the sense of the line is received.

WORDPLAY

That last example introduces another linguistic feature of the play. Juliet's line was clearly written by a man who was alive to the ambiguities of words, the different senses they carry, and who wished to use these senses.

Shakespeare often carries on several meanings at once; his language is **multivocal** (speaking with more than one voice) or **multivalent** (having more than one meaning). He delights in ambiguities, in the connotations and nuances of words. Particularly in an early play like *Romeo and Juliet* there is a kind of exuberance, of abandon, in the manipulation of words. The text abounds with examples of the rhetorical and **metaphorical** ingenuity which the Elizabethans applauded as 'witty writing'. (**Elizabethan wit** conveyed far more than humour, though this might be part of its effect; it contained the idea of surprise and unexpectedness, with a touch of fantasticality. In modern English it might be rendered as clever inventiveness, ingenious dexterity). This can be very disconcerting for a modern reader unaccustomed to this taste for elaboration, repetition, puns, paradoxes, **conceits**.

This is most immediately evident in the wordplay in which everyone in *Romeo and Juliet* indulges. Characters quibble with words, play with their senses, make puns, from the very first lines of the play, when the servants talk about 'coals', 'collier', 'choler' and 'collar', until its end, when the Prince speaks of heaven finding means 'to kill your joys with love' and of a 'glooming peace' (V.3.293, 305). Unfamiliarity with the vocabulary and literary manner makes it very difficult to follow such a 'wit combat' as Romeo and Mercutio's in II.4. Mercutio is the character most adept at playing with double meanings. Romeo cannot say the simplest thing without Mercutio twisting it. Romeo, though, can do it too. When Mercutio observes that 'dreamers often lie', that is that they tell lies, Romeo wittily follows by taking 'lie' in the sense 'lie down' when he says 'In bed asleep, while they do dream things true'. Mercutio had made a complete statement; Romeo uses it as merely the introduction to his own point, which is the opposite of Mercutio's. And he does this simply by a play on the word 'lie' (I.4.51–2).

What is the point of such wordplay? Part of the answer is that in the pun, the quibble, double meanings and the like, Shakespeare was displaying his skill. He was a professional writer, responding to the taste of his audience (and, we may conjecture, himself). Elizabethans greatly appreciated this kind of linguistic ingenuity. The love poetry of John Donne, written at the same time as *Romeo and Juliet*, is characterised by the same kind of exhibitionist wordplay. The intention is to call attention to the writing itself. In that respect, the text of *Romeo and Juliet* is not a means to an end. It is not simply the medium by which the characters speak and the action is realised. It is itself an end, to be enjoyed for its own sake, regardless of what it conveys about character or plot.

Modern taste can accept the comic use of the pun but can be disconcerted when Shakespeare indulges in verbal ingenuity at serious moments. Sometimes it is very hard to see how the puns in such cases contribute to the effect. When Juliet is saying goodbye to Romeo she puns on the word 'division' (III.5.29–30). Her feelings are genuine in this passage, but to modern taste the wordplay introduces a note of false ingenuity.

In some serious moments, though, it is clear how the wordplay contributes to the effect. It may produce powerful compression of language: much is said in little space. For example, when the Prince says 'Throw your mistempered weapons to the ground' (I.1.87), he means that the weapons are badly tempered (or made) because they are used in bad temper by fellow citizens against each other. Or it may express confusion of feeling: when Juliet fears Romeo is dead, she puns on the pronoun 'I', the vowel 'i', the eye and the word 'ay' (III.2.45–50). Her lines effectively convey the fact that if Romeo is dead she too ceases to exist as a person, as a distinct 'I'. Later in this scene, Juliet strings together a list of **oxymorons** (III.2.75–6). The verbal conflict in these words of opposite meanings reflects Juliet's emotional conflict: she loves Romeo and yet is appalled at what he has done in killing Tybalt. In III.5, after Romeo has left, Lady Capulet comes to speak to Juliet. She believes Juliet grieves for the death of Tybalt, though we know Juliet is actually grieving for Romeo's departure. The two understandings are kept in play throughout the dialogue, Juliet meaning one thing and Lady Capulet taking a different meaning. Here, the verbal ingenuity underlines the gulf between mother and daughter. They are not talking to each other at all. Lady Capulet has no notion of what her daughter really means or any understanding of her true feelings, and this the audience realises since it does understand what Juliet means (III.5.68–102).

THE LANGUAGE OF LOVE

A different aspect of this delight in language is Shakespeare's use of the conventional diction of love poetry. We have noticed that Mercutio jests at

Romeo as a follower of **Petrarch** (see Love of Romeo and Juliet), and in the early scenes Romeo is forever using an exaggerated form of the artificial language of Renaissance love poetry. The implication of the **hyperbole** (exaggeration) and contrivance of his speeches in I.1 and I.2 is that his feelings for Rosaline do not run very deep. (In a similar way, the over-obvious rhetorical patterning of the laments in IV.5.49–64 prevents us from taking them too seriously.)

But Shakespeare can use the conventions of love poetry to quite a different purpose. The **sonnet** was then the most popular form for love poetry. Sir Philip Sidney's sequence of sonnets *Astrophel and Stella* (1591) started a vogue, almost a craze. Every poet (including Shakespeare himself) turned out love sonnets during the last decade of the sixteenth century and the first of the seventeenth century. Shakespeare uses this form in all seriousness in the play. When Romeo and Juliet first meet, their conversation is in the form of an **Elizabethan (or Shakespearean) sonnet**. This usually rhymed abab cdcd efef gg, although this example (1.5.93–106) repeats the second rhyme of the first **quatrain** to give abab cbcb dede ff. The closing **couplet** brings it to a final climax. This sonnet gives to the meeting that the audience has been expecting a formality and dignity, as well as an elevating and lyrical quality. Just as the form of the sonnet is completed in the final couplet, so the meeting comes to a climax, the courtship is completed, and the lovers kiss.

This is, clearly, a carefully designed 'set piece'. There are a number of other such set pieces in the play, carefully written speeches, which may strike modern taste as a little over-long. Examples are Mercutio's Queen Mab speech (I.4.53–95); Juliet's **soliloquies** as she waits for news of Romeo and as she prepares to take the potion (III.2.1–31; IV.3.14–59); the Friar's first soliloquy, his long speech to Romeo on moderation and patience, his explanation of his plan and his summary of the plot (II.3.1–26; III.3.108–58; IV.1.89–120; V.3.229–69); and Romeo's soliloquy as he prepares for death (V.3.74–120). Here we are again confronted with the fact that this is not realistic drama but poetic drama, addressed to an audience who appreciated verse. The way to respond to such pieces is not to ask whether people in this situation would really have talked like this; nor is it to ask whether the point made needs to be made at such length. These are not prose passages conveying only meaning, but passages which, though poetry, seek to create a certain mood or response to what is

THE LANGUAGE OF LOVE continued

happening. They are the Elizabethan equivalent of the photographic and sound effects a modern film producer uses to persuade his audience to respond in a certain way to his film.

STYLISTIC VARIETY

Something of the variety of Shakespeare's style in the play is beginning to emerge. We have noticed:
> The use of colloquial idioms
> Punning for comic effect
> Wordplay for serious dramatic effect
> The use of the conventional language of love poetry, both mockingly and in earnest
> Elaborate soliloquies and long speeches
> To these we may add:

THE USE OF PROSE

Shakespeare always used prose for comic characters and characters of a low position in society. So the servants, Gregory and Sampson, begin the play in prose. It obviously distinguishes them from the noble and more important characters who speak in more expressive and dignified verse. Prose is also used to show changes of feeling and mood. The comic banter at the beginning of II.4 is in prose, but later in the scene when, in more serious mood, Romeo plans his marriage, he speaks in verse. In II.5 the Nurse moves in and out of prose according to the tone of her speech; when she finally gets to the important matter of Romeo's message, she settles on verse.

THE USE OF RHYME

There is far more rhyme in this early play than in Shakespeare's later work. With the passage of time he came to use **blank verse** (unrhymed lines of five stresses) almost exclusively. Rhymed verse obviously sounds more artificial than unrhymed (we notice the rhymes), and it limits the poet, who has to find a rhyming word at the end of each line. In *Romeo and Juliet* the rhyme is often incidental, but in II.3, for example, its use throughout the scene serves to remove the world of the Friar and his cell from the rest of the play, where people do not use rhyme so consistently. Rhyme may mark out key statements (for example, III.1.119–20), and its formality of tone is used to distinguish important moments in the action, for example, when Romeo first sees Juliet (I.5.44–53) and the ending of the play. It may also register a decisive change in the action: so, when Romeo leaves Juliet, it is with a **couplet** (III.5.58–9). In all these cases (and many others) the rhyming words signal that something significant is happening at that moment.

SUITING OF LANGUAGE TO CHARACTER

The formality of Escalus's speeches may be contrasted with Mercutio's wit, and both of these with the Nurse's colloquial and wandering utterances. Similarly, variety in the language expresses the different moods of a character: in I.2 Capulet speaks calmly, but his disjointed speech towards the end of III.5 effectively conveys the heat of his emotions.

IMAGERY

Romeo and Juliet is remarkable for the evocative power of its imagery. This is another aspect of that delight in words mentioned earlier, and again marks out the play as an early work. There is an extraordinary richness in its figurative language. This is especially noticeable in the balcony scene, II.2, but it is there, in a different mood, in Juliet's **soliloquy** in IV.3 and as Romeo prepares for death in V.3. Shakespeare can conjure up exquisite beauty and horrible death, the beautiful and the grotesque, with equally vivid imagery. The **metaphors** can also be more subtle: Lady Capulet's elaborate comparison of Paris to a book sounds impossibly far-fetched and contrived, and so reflects the insincerity of her feelings. She is not really interested in Paris as a person at all. She wants to 'sell' Paris to Juliet as a highly desirable husband (I.3.80–95).

WORDS AND TRUTH

There is one way in which language impinges upon the themes of the play. Throughout his career Shakespeare was intrigued by the relationship between words and truth. Often in his plays elaborate and involved language is associated with hypocrisy and deceit, plain speaking with honesty and truthfulness. In *King Lear*, for example, the daughters Goneril and Regan, who do not love their father Lear, speak to him in ornate and contrived speeches; the third daughter, Cordelia, who does love him, speaks plainly and directly. The nobleman, Kent, who sides with Cordelia when Lear casts her off, also speaks bluntly and plainly; the courtier Oswald, who sides with Goneril in her quarrel with the King, speaks in the fashionable language of the court. When Lear himself comes to realise the truth, he too speaks plainly (*King Lear*, I.1.34–187; II.2.1–122; IV.7.1–85.)

Although an early play, *Romeo and Juliet* shows something of the same bias. Mercutio mocks Romeo for adopting the language of love poetry (II.4.38–43; see Love of Romeo and Juliet), and Mercutio similarly mocks as false the assumed language of fashionable courtiers (II.4.28–35). The Friar makes a similar point. When Romeo comes to tell him of his new love for Juliet, the Friar loses patience with Romeo's elaborate **metaphorical** language, and begs Romeo, 'Be plain, good son, and homely in thy drift. / Riddling confession finds but riddling shrift' (II.3.51–2). At this Romeo at last gives over his **conceits**, and speaks directly: 'Then plainly know my heart's dear love is set / On the fair daughter of rich Capulet' (II.3.53–4). And the Friar suggests Rosaline had rejected Romeo precisely because his affected talk of love was seen by her as insincere, something memorised specially for the occasion: 'O, she knew well / Thy love did read by rote, that could not spell' (II.3.83–4).

Above all, though, it is Juliet who is suspicious of words. In the balcony scene she rejects the affected language of courtship, that is, language which does not tell the truth about one's feelings ('farewell compliment' (II.2.89)); she beseeches Romeo to speak plainly ('O gentle Romeo / If thou dost love, pronounce it faithfully' (II.2.93–4)); and she stops Romeo swearing an elaborate lover's oath (II.2.109–11). Her frankness here reflects her sincere and unaffected feelings. Later in the play, there is a clear contrast between Romeo, still inclined to be fanciful, and Juliet. As they are about to be married, Romeo asks Juliet to describe their love, as he cannot do it:

> Ah, Juliet, if the measure of thy joy
> Be heaped like mine, and that thy skill be more
> To blazon it, then sweeten with thy breath
> This neighbour air, and let rich music's tongue
> Unfold the imagined happiness that both
> Receive in either by this dear encounter. (II.6.24–9)

Romeo's language here – 'blazon', 'rich music's tongue' – shows the kind of thing he has in mind. Juliet, however, replies:

> Conceit, more rich in matter than in words,
> Brags of his substance, not of ornament.
> They are but beggars that can count their worth.
> But my true love is grown to such excess
> I cannot sum up sum of half my wealth. (II.6.30–4)

Juliet is saying here that words, however elaborate, cannot possibly convey what she feels; and that she values the thing itself (her love) more than the ability to describe it. In other words, she sees Romeo's invitation as a pointless exercise. This distrust of fine-sounding words to convey anything truly will be a recurring theme in later plays.

CHARACTERISATION

THE GROUPING OF THE CHARACTERS

The action of *Romeo and Juliet* involves two carefully balanced groups of characters. At the head of the two feuding families of Verona are Lord and Lady Capulet and Lord and Lady Montague. Juliet, not yet fourteen years old (I.2.9; I.3.11–15), is the only child and heir of the Capulets (I.2.14; I.5.112–7), as the youthful Romeo is of the Montagues (we hear of no other children, and V.3.210–11 suggests Romeo is an only son). As Juliet has a cousin, Tybalt (I.5.61; III.2.66, 96), so Benvolio is Romeo's cousin (I.1.105, 159; II.1.3). These two cousins are clearly contrasted. When we first meet them, Tybalt starts a fight and Benvolio tries to keep the peace (I.1.63–71). This is characteristic. Throughout the play, the 'fiery Tybalt' (I.1.109) feels resentment and anger, while, on the other hand, Benvolio tries to prevent quarrelling and fighting (for example III.1.1–4, 49–52). And, as the hero and heroine each have a cousin, so each has a close friend. Juliet's foster-mother and confidante, the Nurse, is balanced by Romeo's friend, Mercutio. Just as the old, easy-going and talkative Nurse is a contrast to the young and quiet Juliet, so the witty, intelligent and high-spirited Mercutio is a contrast to the passionate and often depressed Romeo.

The ruler of Verona, Prince Escalus, is set apart from both families, but his public commands to the two families to cease their feuding (I.1.81–103; III.1.186–97) are paralleled in their turn by Friar Laurence's secret attempts to unite Capulets and Montagues through the marriage of Romeo and Juliet (II.3.85–8). Outside each family, the Prince in public and the Friar in secret try to prevent that hostility which, in the end, kills Romeo and Juliet. The Prince as a ruler is concerned to stop 'mutiny' amongst his subjects, and the Friar, as a churchman, is also led by his office to try to stop it, but, although the Prince and the Friar are outside the families, each is connected to both, and so involved in their quarrelling personally: the Prince as the kinsman of Romeo's friend Mercutio and Juliet's suitor Paris (V.3.295; III.1.109, 145, 188–9) and the Friar as father-confessor to both Romeo and Juliet (II.2.192; II.4.177–9).

And finally, all these noble figures are off-set by the servants of each household – it is, indeed, with the servants quarrelling in comic imitation of their masters that the play begins.

Clearly, the characters are not a casual collection of people, but figures brought together as part of a design, carefully arranged in contrasting groups. They are constructed not as people but as parts of a dramatic pattern. It is no accident that Shakespeare develops Mercutio and the Nurse from his source (see Shakespeare's Use of Sources): he needs them as part of his design. Though Shakespeare's characters are marvellously credible beings, realistic, it might be said, caution must be exercised in thinking about them as people. Their primary purpose is theatrical, not psychological or realistic. Their neat arrangement in pairs and as foils to each other does not reflect 'real life'; it is dramatically contrastive and thematically revealing. So Juliet's youth and innocence are made clearer by the Nurse's age and rather immoral worldly wisdom; Benvolio's peaceable nature is made plainer by Tybalt's quarrelsomeness. And Shakespeare gains dramatic effect by constantly varying the pattern: Tybalt clashes with Benvolio in I.1, but with Mercutio and Romeo in III.1. We see Juliet not only with the Nurse, but with Romeo, with Lady Capulet, with her father, with the Friar. Each time she is presented in a new light.

It is to fulfil their roles in the dramatic design that the characters each have a typical quality. Thus, the Prince is there primarily as a figure of authority and stability. He represents order – that order in society which the feud of Capulets and Montagues threatens. If we understand this, then we can see why it is fitting that it is the Prince who officially oversees the reconciliation of the families at the end of the play. His presence enforces the fact that order and harmony have been restored. A similar kind of general quality is present in all the characters: Romeo is the young lover; the Nurse the old gossip; the Friar the secret schemer whom Protestant Elizabethan England loved to imagine as typical of Roman Catholic Italy.

This is not to say that Shakespeare does not individualise his characters. He certainly does. The following notes indicate something of their individuality, but yet they remain parts of the play, not human beings whom we can imagine meeting anywhere other than in the theatre.

Romeo

Romeo first appears as a moody rejected lover, given to elaborate complaint about the pain caused by a love we suspect is not very deep (see Love of Romeo and Juliet, and The Language of Love). But he had not always been solitary and withdrawn like this. The very fact that his father, Benvolio and Mercutio all make so much of his changed 'humour' shows that his present behaviour is a drastic alteration and that he is not like the Romeo they used to know (I.1.118–57; I.4). He is well thought of in Verona. Even Capulet, the head of the rival house, admits it (I.5.65–8). He says that Romeo is 'well-governed': clearly, Romeo was not always subject to such moods. The implication is that, before he became infatuated with Rosaline, Romeo was a popular, lively and sociable member of Veronese society.

It is therefore a testimony to the truth of his feelings for Juliet that, when he has arranged his marriage to her, he is like his old self. 'Now art thou sociable. Now art thou Romeo,' exclaims Mercutio (II.4.87). Whereas the infatuation with Rosaline dulled him, Romeo's love for Juliet reveals his true liveliness. By this simple change, Shakespeare comments on the nature of the affections and, in Romeo's high spirits in II.4, shows us how witty he really is.

Once he has ceased to brood, however, Romeo is clearly rather impractical. He is all for impetuous action, but takes little consideration as to ways and means. Juliet has to point out to him that the marriage must be arranged; he is more inclined to express the rapture of his love than to plan what to do about it (II.2.139–48, 164–9). When he goes to the Friar, he is in a great hurry, but has no real suggestion to make beyond saying the

Friar 'must' marry them (II.3.53–60). Later, when he meets the angry Tybalt, Romeo is at first moderate, but the death of Mercutio is too much for him: 'fire-eyed fury be my conduct now,' he cries (III.1.124) and he throws consideration to the winds.

Impetuous and impractical, Romeo is also more than a little passionate, as that last example suggests. When he hears of his banishment, he behaves very much like a child, throwing himself to the ground in a frenzy of grief (III.3.65–71, 84). He has here lost all self-control. It is the Friar who brings him to himself and shows him what he now must do (III.3.109–59). It is entirely characteristic that when, in Mantua, he hears the news of Juliet's death, he reacts immediately, without waiting a moment to consider what is the best thing to do. As he rushed into marriage, collapsed into grief, so now he decides instantly to return to Verona to kill himself (V.1.24–6).

The passion and impetuosity that lurk in Romeo are his most distinctive features, and, to an extent, they are responsible for the tragedy which overwhelms the lovers. Had he been a little less hasty, less impassioned, all would have been well. A little delay in V.1 would have given time for him to learn the truth about Juliet's 'death'. On the other hand, it is this same quality which allows him to give himself so entirely and completely to Juliet. It is characteristic of Shakespeare that the same trait is at once the thing we admire and the thing we regret, both a source of strength and of fallibility.

JULIET

Juliet is a much quieter character than Romeo. She begins the play as a submissive and obedient girl who has lived a sheltered life and in the course of the play develops into a resolute woman (see Love of Romeo and Juliet). Romeo's character does not so much change: rather, we find out what he is really like. But Juliet does change, and the mature Juliet is a contrast to the impassioned Romeo. Her love is as deep as his, and as deeply felt (notice how she longs for the return of the Nurse at the beginning of II.5, and anticipates her wedding night in III.2). There is nothing insipid or weak about her feelings, but she has more awareness of the practicalities of the situation than Romeo and she speaks much more frankly (see Words and Truth).

She contrasts with Romeo in another way, too. There was an element of self-deceit in Romeo's role as Rosaline's lover. Juliet, as her plain speaking shows, is above all honest, with both Romeo and herself. Because of Romeo's banishment she is reduced to playing a part, the part designed for her in the Friar's plan. But she never becomes less than true to herself. Deception is not her nature, and nothing less than her love for Romeo would have prompted her to deceive her parents. That she does so is a measure not of how deceitful she is but of how independent and firm-minded she has become. She recognises only one obligation – to Romeo.

This aspect of her character is enforced by the fact that she is gradually isolated from everyone she knows and loves. This, indeed, happens to Romeo too, but he is away in Mantua throughout Act IV and it is Juliet whom we actually see struggling alone with circumstances. She is without Romeo; cut off from her parents because they do not know of her marriage; even the Nurse lets her down by suggesting bigamy when Juliet turns to her for help (III.5.213–26). Juliet is thus abandoned by everyone in the one scene, III.5, which begins with Romeo's departure. These repeated desertions are cumulatively very striking. Juliet's exclamation 'Ancient damnation!' (III.5.236) marks the final break with all the guardians of her childhood. She is now alone, a tragic heroine: 'My dismal scene I needs must act alone' (IV.3.19).

FRIAR LAURENCE

The Friar is the one person to whom Romeo and Juliet can both turn throughout the play. Everyone speaks well of him, and his is the voice of moderation in a stormy and violent world (see Competing Views of Love – Passion and Moderation). He is a pleasant and likeable figure, but not a very complex one. He is chiefly important as the means to promote the plot. As a character he will not sustain serious interrogation: should he have agreed to a secret marriage? should he have deceived Juliet's parents? don't his words to them in their grief when they think Juliet is dead sound like hypocrisy – he is certainly not telling the truth (IV.5.65–83)? doesn't he treat Juliet's parents cruelly, putting them through this suffering? These questions might be asked of a real friar: they cannot be asked of Friar Laurence, for there are no answers provided in the text. The Prince's verdict that he is a holy man (V.3.270) has to be accepted as a convention of the play, however much we might wonder what kind of holiness it is that can do what Friar Laurence does. In a case like this, talk of the realism of Shakespeare's characters can only mislead.

Juliet herself comes up against this difficulty. As she is about to take the potion, she raises moral questions about the Friar, that is, she treats him as a real human being with motives for his actions. She wonders whether, as he has already married her secretly to Romeo, he has actually given her poison to take so that she will die and no-one will know what he has done. This suspicion might well be entertained of a real friar who had acted like Friar Laurence. But Juliet puts aside the worry with the rather unconvincing reflection that he must be a holy man:

> What if it be a poison which the Friar
> Subtly hath ministered to have me dead,
> Lest in this marriage he should be dishonoured
> Because he married me before to Romeo?
> I fear it is. And yet methinks it should not,
> For he hath still been tried a holy man. (IV.3.24–9)

Juliet here uses almost the same words as the Prince in the last scene of the play, reasserting the type that the Friar represents. At this moment in this early play a tendency towards greater psychological complexity can be discerned: the Friar has been used as a plot device, but the character of Juliet, though the type of the innocent heroine, has developed a richer inner life which leads her to think about the Friar as an actual person might. This results in a tension between a believable being, who asks questions, and a type figure whose behaviour is determined not by psychological **verisimilitude** but by the demands of his role.

MERCUTIO

Mercutio is important in the play as a foil to Romeo and as a source of comedy, but, much more fully developed than the Friar, he is also a winning personality in himself. Vivacious, lively, always talking, jesting even in death (III.1.96–9), he is a clear contrast to Romeo, but his is an independent mind such that he wins our attention in his own right. He offers us an attitude to love worth considering (see Competing Views of Love – Spiritual and Sexual Love) and, although always witty, his wit is not empty. Mercutio always has a point to make. The thrust of a good many of his jokes against Romeo early in the play wins assent, and his caustic comments on Italian duels and fashionable courtiers mark him out as one whose repartee is based on acute observation (II.4.19–35). Even so, his intelligence and shrewdness do not prevent him from being killed. It was noted earlier that Shakespeare brings Mercutio into the duel in III.1 in order to show Romeo's unwillingness to fight (see Themes – The Feud), but this incident also shows Mercutio has deep feelings, and, what is more, feelings that can be misguided. In so assiduously pursuing the feud, in feeling Romeo has 'let the side down' by refusing to fight Tybalt, Mercutio shows a false sense of honour which, **ironically**, will contribute to the death of his friend. Mercutio had seemed to turn the play into a comedy at times: it is with his death that we know this is to be a tragedy.

THE NURSE

The Nurse is Juliet's equivalent of Romeo's Mercutio. Like Mercutio, she does not change or develop; like him, she supplies a good deal of humour; like him, she has an attitude to love which contrasts with that of the hero and heroine (see Spiritual and Sexual Love); and, like Mercutio, she is almost entirely Shakespeare's invention, being barely mentioned in the sources.

Vulgar, coarse, quite insensitive and immoral, she can be made to sound like an old witch. Her wordiness can be very infuriating. She speaks a good deal and says very little (notice how long it takes her to say how old Juliet is in I.3 and to tell Romeo what she has come for in II.4). This can sometimes seem like a deliberate wilfulness: in II.5 she seems to have little regard for Juliet's feelings as she delays giving Romeo's message. Her garrulousness is a clear contrast to Juliet's unequivocal directness. When Juliet has something to say, she says it directly (with these examples from the Nurse we might compare Juliet's speech to the Friar in IV.1.50–67).

The Nurse contrasts with Juliet in another way, too. Once she has met Romeo, Juliet knows exactly what she thinks and what she wants. The Nurse, on the other hand, changes her mind with bewildering rapidity. She seems to support Lady Capulet in her praise of Paris (I.3.79), and then helps Juliet arrange her marriage to Romeo (II.4). After Tybalt's death, she agrees when Juliet, in her astonishment, raves against Romeo as deceitful

(III.2.85–90); but when Juliet recovers herself, the Nurse readily undertakes to bring Romeo to her (III.2.138–41). She warns Romeo and Juliet of the approach of Lady Capulet in III.5, and yet, at the end of that scene, she much prefers Paris to Romeo ('Romeo's a dishclout to him') and suggests Juliet should marry Paris (III.5.213–26). And although she helped to bring about the marriage to Romeo, she is quite happy to wake Juliet in IV.5 for her marriage to Paris. In short, the Nurse agrees with whatever seems to be the opinion of the moment.

And yet this is not all there is to the Nurse. Certainly, sex, child rearing and old memories make up a good deal of her conversation. She is quite without refinement, but she is also without affectation. She speaks plainly of the basic things of life she knows. To dismiss her as a meddle-some old woman, however, is to be less sympathetic than Shakespeare, who has given her an obviously genuine love for Juliet (for example in I.3.60–3) and a position of trust in the Capulet household. It is sad that she lets Juliet down at the crucial time (III.5.205–43), but she can hardly be blamed for that. She is advising what seems to her, truly, to be the best course of action, and, although she does not know it, she is more than punished by losing Juliet's confidence. This is something that would hurt her deeply. Indeed, that the Nurse does not understand the depth of Juliet's love for Romeo, and so can suggest marriage to Paris, is a measure of how far Juliet has grown up. She is no longer a little girl whom the Nurse can influence; now she is a woman with a commitment beyond the Nurse's comprehension.

LORD AND LADY CAPULET

See Competing Views of Love for a discussion of their role.

BENVOLIO AND TYBALT

These simple characters, the peacemaker and the quarreller, are obvious contrasts. They behave according to type throughout the play, and have none of the liveliness or individuality of Mercutio or the Nurse. Tybalt is always angry (I.1.65–71; I.5.54–92; III.1.34–132; these are the only times he appears in the play). He believes it is up to him to keep the quarrel alive. He takes Romeo's appearance at the party as a personal insult and deter-mines to avenge it. By contrast, Capulet and Montague, the older men, seem inclined to let the quarrel drop (for example in I.2.1–3; I.5.54–88).

Benvolio concerns us a little more, as the friend who persuades Romeo to say why he is so depressed. But thereafter he is always for peace, and rather overshadowed by Mercutio and Tybalt. He is clearly a foil to them, and so vanishes from the play after III. 1. With both Mercutio and Tybalt dead, Benvolio is no longer needed as part of the design. That Shakespeare is so willing simply to drop a character from the play, without explanation, shows that he is thinking in terms of design, in terms of the usefulness of the characters.

PARIS

Paris is not the unpleasant character we might expect the hero's rival to be, but he is very different from Romeo. Whereas Romeo is passionate and impetuous, Paris is calm and decorous. He acts as a suitor to a young lady ought to act. Against Romeo's impetuosity, he offers us the normal form of courtship. He does not steal into the lady's garden at night, nor does he visit her room secretly. He approaches her father with a proper proposal (I.2), and, when the father offers him his daughter's hand, he accepts it, even though he knows the daughter has not been asked (III.4). Indeed, it seems that Paris has never even spoken to Juliet: all his wooing has been to Capulet. (By contrast, Romeo has spoken only to Juliet, not to her father.) Thus, Paris serves to exemplify a very different kind of love from Romeo's. His proper course of courtship seems a rather pallid thing. His affection lacks passionate involvement, and, in paying scant heed to Juliet's own wishes ('That "may be" must be, love, on Thursday next' (IV.1.20)), seems to lack respect for the loved one.

But we should not be too hard on Paris. Shakespeare, clearly, could not develop Paris's love too much, or the audience would have been distracted from Romeo and would have begun to see Juliet as torn between two equally eligible young men. As it is, we see a different kind of love offered, and one which, though it may seem pale beside Romeo's, is not necessarily insincere. When Paris does meet Juliet in IV.1 he treats her with some consideration and tenderness, and his obsequies in V.2 suggest a genuine affection. And, like Romeo, he wishes to lie with Juliet in death (V.3.72–3). Furthermore, his courage in V.3, when he fights Romeo, should prevent his being dismissed as a weak and unfeeling person.

PART FOUR

TEXTUAL ANALYSIS

TEXT 1   THE NURSE REMINISCES (I.3.17–49)

Even or odd, of all days in the year,
Come Lammas Eve at night shall she be fourteen.

...

I never should forget it. 'Wilt thou not, Jule?' quoth he,
And, pretty fool, it stinted and said 'Ay'.

The Nurse and Mercutio are the two chief sources of comic energy in the play. The comedy they provide is of very different kinds. Whereas Mercutio is a verbal gamester, all mercurial wit, the Nurse is garrulously repetitive and digressive. Though he can speak at length (as in his famous Queen Mab speech, I.4.53–95), Mercutio's characteristic manner is that of quick repartee, the swift riposte. He is a master of wordplay and the deft retort, but the Nurse can never clear-sightedly get to the point: she infuriates Juliet with her inability to say anything directly and straightforwardly (for example, when she returns from Romeo in II.5). Her tendency to prolong whatever she is saying by wandering from the point, adding details, repeating herself, is well illustrated by this speech, but it illustrates also the fact that the Nurse's role in the play is not merely to supply comic relief from the tragic story of the lovers. She provides both a context for that story, and a dramatically striking and thematically revealing contrast to the experience and perceptions of Romeo and Juliet.

In the first of these functions, she keeps before the audience the everyday facts of life. Romeo and Juliet are caught up in an exceptional love, prompting them to disregard the normal constraints on human behaviour. They take no care of any obligation save that of fidelity to each other. In the end, even the most fundamental human desire – to survive – has no hold on them. While they thus escape from all the ties of family and society, the Nurse is entirely caught up in them. Her speech is replete with the ordinary, inconsequential events which compose most human lives: for her, they are all that does constitute life. This is evident in her insistent references to time. Time is one thing Romeo and Juliet disregard. In their love affair, normal temporal sequences and expectations seem suspended: they fall in love when they are too young to do so, they marry before they have known each other more than a day, their marriage is over in a day. Their love is at once timeless, and moves at great speed. Their scenes together seem to be removed from the normal world, even though compelled by the onward rush of events.

This effect is sustained in large part by the Nurse. She brings noise and bustle on to the stage ('hold thy peace' says the exasperated Lady Capulet in response to this speech), which, by contrast, makes the scenes between the lovers appear the calmer and quieter – havens of peacefulness. The absolute single-mindedness of the lovers and their clarity of purpose is the more striking because of the Nurse's complete lack of focus or purposefulness. She wants to chat, not to do. Whereas Romeo and Juliet seem driven by fate, the Nurse appears to have all the time in the world (she is certainly in no hurry here) and (at least until Juliet's apparent death) nothing to worry her. And yet the Nurse also reminds us insistently of time, but it is a time-scale quite different to that which affects Romeo and Juliet. In this speech, she ticks off days, months and years. Her life spans a long stretch of time, but it is a stretch marked out by birth, marriage and death (all are mentioned in this speech, which moves from Juliet's birth and weaning to her marriage, with mention of the death of the Nurse's own daughter and her husband); by Christian festivals (Lammastide); by natural events (the earthquake); and by ordinary domestic duties (weaning a child) and events (a child falling over), and household exchanges (her husband's joke). Her speech is larded with inconsequential details ('sitting in the sun under the dovehouse wall', for example) which, though irrelevant (or, at least, not necessary) to what she is saying, create an everyday world never encountered in the lives of the lovers. Ordinariness, the keynote of the Nurse's experience, highlights, by contrast, the extraordinariness which characterises Romeo and Juliet's love. Her speech keeps the play rooted in the world of the audience's experience and epitomises the life that Romeo and Juliet will never have.

And as she talks of these things, she exemplifies values which are quite at odds with those of the hero and heroine. Her whole speech revolves around a joke about sex. She clearly enjoys the joke hugely, just as she does sex. The love of Romeo and Juliet is certainly sexual, but their tone is never like this. They speak of and to each other with a kind of awe, as though

TEXT 1 continued

what is happening to them is almost beyond belief. The Nurse's tone is colloquially familiar, with its everyday diction ('dug', 'tetchy'), exclamations ('by my holidam', 'by th'rood'), affectionate terms ('pretty fool'), digressions, conversational idioms ('I do bear a brain', 'Twas no need, I trow, / To bid me trudge') and phrases ('That shall she, marry!', ''A was a merry man'). Just so her attitudes are entirely down to earth. She sees nothing indecorous in talking about (and talking to her social superior about) the details of weaning, nor in contemplating Juliet in bed with a man. Whereas Romeo can apostrophise both love and death in elaborate speeches, the Nurse is matter-of-fact about, and conventional in her response to, death ('She was too good for me') and reduces love to a sexual encounter (the 'jest' is now 'come about' because in marriage Juliet will lie upon her back).

And yet even here we are reminded of the ominous fate brooding over the lovers. Earthquakes were regarded by Elizabethans as portents of dire events, and that earthquake which shakes the dovecote and makes the Nurse run in with Juliet would have alarmed the audience with its intimation of catastrophe in the future. Its incongruous appearance here, amongst so much that is trivial, is the more disturbing.

TEXT 2   FIRST MEETING OF ROMEO AND JULIET (I.5.93–144)

ROMEO

If I profane with my unworthiest hand
This holy shrine, the gentle sin is this.

…

NURSE

Anon, anon!
Come, let's away. The strangers all are gone.

Romeo has been persuaded, rather against his will, to attend the Capulet party by Mercutio, who hopes that the sight of other women will shake Romeo from his infatuation with Rosaline. At the end of the previous scene, Romeo's misgivings found expression in one of the play's many speeches of dire portent (I.4.106–13), but in his next speech, far from foreseeing his 'untimely death', he is stunned by the effect upon him of his first sight of Juliet (I.5.44–53). He resolves to speak to her, and when he does so it is in the tones of adoration and with the religious imagery which he had used at line 51. He presents himself as a pilgrim approaching the shrine of a saint. This was not at all an uncommon construction in the love poetry of the time which made ready use of religious imagery. Following **Petrarch**, the woman was frequently depicted as saint, angel, or goddess, whom the male suitor approaches with expression of his unworthiness and undeserving. The rhetoric of the poetry supposes that it is the woman's part to confer blessing, mercy, grace upon the man by answering his prayer or plea. Equally conventional is the **sonnet** form upon which Romeo here embarks (see Tragedy – Fate and Chance). Language, genre and imagery are all at this point telling the audience that this is a moment of true love.

What is not conventional is the mutuality of the exchange. Ordinarily in love poetry it is the male voice that is heard; the woman may be adored, but, almost without exception, she remains silent (the poetry of John Donne illustrates this). Curiously, while the poetry appears to elevate woman, it actually deprives her of any real presence. Even in plays, the woman's role is commonly subordinate to that of the man. In Shakespeare's *Much Ado About Nothing*, for example, Claudio is allowed a voice but the woman he loves, Hero, is silent for almost the entire play. When she does speak, it is in the role of a subordinate woman, utterly at the mercy of male perceptions. In this passage, the situation is quite different. Not only does Juliet speak but she addresses Romeo as an equal.

The point is made by the structure of the dialogue. The **sonnet** upon which Romeo embarks is taken up by Juliet. They compose it together, each having first a **quatrain,** and then an exchange of lines (not quite equally, in fact; Juliet has three lines to Romeo's six). During this exchange, the image introduced by Romeo is developed by them both, with Juliet showing herself Romeo's equal in wit. She deftly turns aside his request for a kiss with the reflection that religious devotion is satisfied with touching the statue of a saint and with hands clasped in prayer, and that it is in prayer that lips express love (lines 97–102). When Romeo responds with the request that she 'let lips do what hands do', namely, pray by touching, her exquisitely poised and tactful reply turns on a pun on *move* (it was she who had introduced the pun on *palm/palmers*): she may not move to kiss him (anymore than could the statue of a saint) though moved to grant his plea. It is at the fourteenth line of the sonnet, that is, at the completion of the

TEXT 2 continued

pattern the audience, familiar with sonnet form, would have anticipated, that they kiss. With another exchange of wit, turning now on the idea that, as Romeo has purged his sin by this act of devotion, Juliet has now to be cleansed of the sin she has received from him, they are about to kiss when this second sonnet is interrupted by the Nurse.

This exchange has thus established not only the exalted nature of their love, through the religious imagery and the formality of the **sonnet**, but also its mutuality: Romeo and Juliet play equal parts, they share the exchange as they share the experience. This will hold throughout the play: it is never the case that Romeo takes charge; the lovers love, and suffer, together, equally caught up in their affection, equally helpless. That helplessness is impressed upon them immediately, even at this moment of their meeting, for in the following lines each learns the identity of the other's family. It is entirely fitting that it is the Nurse, that epitome of worldliness and the everyday, who is the source of this knowledge: as she comes to them, the world imposes its constraints upon them. The exchange between Benvolio and Romeo at lines 118–20 ominously recalls the tenor of Romeo's earlier prediction (I.4.106–13); it is echoed in Juliet's line, 'My grave is like to be my wedding bed' (line 135), the first of the many associations of love and death in the play (see Tragedy – Juliet as the Bride of Death). Thus, from its first appearance in the play, the love between Romeo and Juliet is marked out not only as exceptional but as doomed, both transcendent and at the mercy of the world. When Juliet says, 'Prodigious birth of love it is to me' (line 140), her words define this moment of meeting in terms both of birth and of death.

TEXT 3   THE FRIAR'S FIRST APPEARANCE (II.3.1–90)

FRIAR

Now, ere the sun avance his burning eye
The day to cheer and night's dank dew to dry,

…

ROMEO

O, let us hence! I stand on sudden haste.

FRIAR

Wisely and slow. They stumble that run fast.

This is the first appearance of the Friar and his opening **soliloquy** strikes the note he will sound throughout the play. He holds to the Elizabethan commonplace that the world constitutes a divinely ordered harmony in which all is structured, ultimately, for good. He believes further that this harmony can be reproduced in human lives if their passions and ambitions are properly tempered. Just as beneficial and malign properties are mingled in plants, so are good and evil inclinations in human beings: 'Two such opposed kings encamp them still / In man as well as herbs – grace and rude will' (lines 23–4). All things, he reflects, can be used for good, but they can also be perverted to evil ends. When the rude will – passion, obsession, overwhelming desire – comes to dominate, the result is disaster. This is exemplified in the Montague/Capulet feud: it threatens to consume people like Tybalt, and does actually kill him and Mercutio (and also Paris, who challenges Romeo as a Montague). Yet Tybalt is not a bad man; he has been 'strained' from his good nature (line 5).

The Friar is thus the spokesperson for moderation and restraint in the play; he holds with a temperate and constant style of life. This is reflected in the quiet, humble task he is here performing, collecting plants early in the morning to make medicines. It is the noisy excess of Romeo's feelings which dismays him later in the scene, as, we learn, it has done in the past. He has, he says, rebuked Romeo 'for doting, not for loving' (line 78), that is, for the obsessiveness of his infatuation. 'They stumble that run fast' are the Friar's characteristic last words in the scene.

This point of view is mirrored in the way, throughout his **soliloquy**, one thought or idea is opposed to, and balanced by, another. Quite often, a line is constructed in two halves, each set against the other: 'With baleful weeds and precious-juicèd flowers' (line 4); 'What is her burying grave, that is her womb' (line 6). More strikingly, the judicious balance which the Friar is trying to maintain is enacted by the **couplets** in which he speaks. The couplet is itself founded on balance, on harmony: one line plays against the other and makes the rhyme. The pattern is completed only when the second line is brought against the first: 'For naught so vile that on the earth doth live / But to the earth some special good doth give' (lines 13–14). In this example, each line contains a single idea, the two ideas appear contradictory, but the rhymed couplet insists that they are equally valid. It binds them together as a single point: the qualities of natural things cannot be distinguished as wholly vile or good.

The continuance of the **couplets** throughout the scene serves to define this location as the Friar's, where Romeo's is an intrusive presence. Though he does not break the couplets, he represents precisely that extremism, that excess, which the Friar disdains. Not only has he veered from one love (Rosaline) to another (Juliet) but he is even more extravagant in his second love than in his first: 'Holy Saint Francis! What a change is here!' (line 61) exclaims the Friar, and in the following lines he rehearses the extravagance of Romeo's earlier protestations and behaviour rather as Mercutio will do in the next scene (see further The Language of Love). The traditional behaviour of the courtly lover is reduced to absurd posturing and histrionic gestures, a matter of flighty performance, not constant commitment.

Even so, the Friar is prepared to countenance this new love in the hope it may reconcile the feuding families (lines 86–8). As this shows, there is a worldly, even political, side to him, which will lead him into plots and contrivances of dubious moral standing. The contrast with Romeo and Juliet is all to their advantage: they have a daring and a courage which is quite beyond him, and it is they, not he, who are the truly unworldly ones, even, in the end, martyrs for their love. He is, of course, right, that, 'running fast', Romeo and Juliet do 'stumble' disastrously, but for all his common sense and prudence, the supreme image of commitment in the play is not the Friar, but the dead lovers. In the end, he is no more use to the lovers, and perhaps understands them no better than the Nurse.

PART FIVE

Background

William shakespeare's life

There are no personal records of Shakespeare's life. Official documents and occasional references to him by contemporary dramatists enable us to draw the main outline of his public life, but his private life remains hidden. Although not at all unusual for a writer of his time, this lack of first-hand evidence has tempted many to read his plays as personal records and to look in them for clues to his character and convictions. The results are unconvincing, partly because Renaissance art was not subjective or designed primarily to express its creator's personality, and partly because the drama of any period is very difficult to read biographically. Except when plays are written by committed dramatists to promote social or political causes (as by Shaw or Brecht), it is all but impossible to decide who amongst the variety of fictional characters in a drama represents the dramatist, or which of the various and often conflicting points of view expressed is authorial.

What we do know can be quickly summarised. Shakespeare was born into a well-to-do family in the market town of Stratford-upon-Avon in Warwickshire, where he was baptised, in Holy Trinity Church, on 26 April 1564. His father, John Shakespeare, was a prosperous glover and leather merchant who became a person of some importance in the town: in 1565 he was elected an alderman, and in 1568 he became high bailiff (or mayor) of Stratford. In 1557 he had married Mary Arden. Their third child (of eight) and eldest son, William, learned to read and write at the primary (or 'petty') school in Stratford and then, it seems probable, attended the local grammar school, where he would have studied Latin, history, logic and rhetoric. In November 1582 William, then aged eighteen, married Anne Hathaway, who was twenty-six years old. They had a daughter, Susanna, in May 1583, and twins, Hamnet and Judith, in 1585.

Shakespeare next appears in the historical record in 1592 when he was mentioned as a London actor and playwright in a pamphlet by the dramatist Robert Greene. These 'lost years' 1585–92 have been the subject of much speculation, but how they were occupied remains as much a mystery as when Shakespeare left Stratford, and why. In his pamphlet,

Greene's Groatsworth of Wit, Greene expresses to his fellow dramatists his outrage that the 'upstart crow' Shakespeare has the impudence to believe he 'is as well able to bombast out a blank verse as the best of you'. To have aroused this hostility from a rival, Shakespeare must, by 1592, have been long enough in London to have made a name for himself as a playwright. We may conjecture that he had left Stratford in 1586 or 1587.

During the next twenty years, Shakespeare continued to live in London, regularly visiting his wife and family in Stratford. He continued to act, but his chief fame was as a dramatist. From 1594 he wrote exclusively for the Lord Chamberlain's Men, which rapidly became the leading dramatic company and from 1603 enjoyed the patronage of James I as the King's Men. His plays were extremely popular and he became a shareholder in his theatre company. He was able to buy lands around Stratford and a large house in the town, to which he retired about 1611. He died there on 23 April 1616 and was buried in Holy Trinity Church on 25 April.

SHAKESPEARE'S DRAMATIC CAREER

Between the late 1580s and 1613 Shakespeare wrote thirty-seven plays, and contributed to some by other dramatists. This was by no means an exceptional number for a professional playwright of the times. The exact date of the composition of individual plays is a matter of debate – for only a few plays is the date of their first performance known – but the broad outlines of Shakespeare's dramatic career have been established. He began in the late 1580s and early 1590s by rewriting earlier plays and working with plotlines inspired by the Classics. He concentrated on comedies (such as *The Comedy of Errors*, 1590–4, which derived from the Latin playwright Plautus) and plays dealing with English history (such as the three parts of *Henry VI*, 1589–92), though he also tried his hand at bloodthirsty revenge tragedy (*Titus Andronicus*, 1592–3, indebted to both Ovid and Seneca). During the 1590s Shakespeare developed his expertise in these kinds of play to write such comic masterpieces such as *A Midsummer Night's Dream* (1594–5) and *As You Like It* (1599–1600) and history plays such as *Henry IV* (1596–8) and *Henry V* (1598–9).

As the new century begins a new note is detectable. Plays such as *Troilus and Cressida* (1601–2) and *Measure for Measure* (1603–4), poised between comedy and tragedy, evoke complex responses. Because of their generic uncertainty and ambivalent tone such works are sometimes referred to as 'problem plays', but it is tragedy which comes to dominate the extraordinary sequence of masterpieces: *Hamlet* (1600–1), *Othello* (1602–4), *King Lear* (1605–6), *Macbeth* (1605–6) and *Antony and Cleopatra* (1606).

In the last years of his dramatic career, Shakespeare wrote a group of plays of a quite different kind. These 'romances', as they are often called, are in many ways the most remarkable of all his plays. The group comprises *Pericles* (1608), *Cymbeline* (1609–11), *The Winter's Tale* (1610–11) and *The Tempest* (1610–11). These plays (particularly *Cymbeline*) reprise many of the situations and themes of the earlier dramas but in fantastical and exotic dramatic designs which, set in distant lands, covering large tracts of time and involving music, mime, dance and tableaux, have something of the qualities of masques and pageants. The situations which in the tragedies had led to disaster are here resolved: the great theme is restoration and reconciliation. Where in the tragedies Ophelia, Desdemona and Cordelia died, the daughters of these plays – Marina, Imogen, Perdita, Miranda – survive and are reunited with their parents and lovers.

The texts of shakespeare's plays

Nineteen of Shakespeare's plays were printed during his lifetime in what are called '**quartos**' (books, each containing one play, and made up of sheets of paper each folded twice to make four leaves). Shakespeare, however, did not supervise their publication. This was not unusual. When a playwright had sold a play to a dramatic company he sold his rights in it: copyright belonged to whoever had possession of an actual copy of the text, and so consequently authors had no control over what happened to their work. Anyone who could get hold of the text of a play might publish it if they wished. Hence, what found its way into print might be the author's copy, but it might be an actor's copy or prompt copy, perhaps cut or altered for performance; sometimes, actors (or even members of the audience) might publish what they could remember of the text. Printers, working without the benefit of the author's oversight, introduced their own errors, through misreading the manuscript for example, and by 'correcting' what seemed to them not to make sense.

In 1623 John Heminges and Henry Condell, two actors in Shakespeare's company, collected together texts of thirty-six of Shakespeare's plays (*Pericles* was omitted) and published them in a large **folio** (a book in which each sheet of paper is folded once in half, to give two leaves). This, the First Folio, was followed by later editions in 1632, 1663 and 1685. Despite its appearance of authority, however, the texts in the First Folio still present many difficulties, for there are printing errors and confused passages in the plays, and its texts often differ significantly from those of the earlier quartos, when these exist.

Shakespeare's texts have, then, been through a number of intermediaries. We do not have his authority for any one of his plays, and hence we cannot know exactly what it was that he wrote. Bibliographers, textual critics and editors have spent a great deal of effort on endeavouring to get behind the errors, uncertainties and contradictions in the available texts to recover the plays as Shakespeare originally wrote them. What we read is the result of these efforts. Modern texts are what editors have constructed from the available evidence: they correspond to no sixteenth- or seventeenth-century editions, and to no early performance of a Shakespeare play. Furthermore, these composite texts differ from each other, for different editors read the early texts differently and come to different conclusions. A Shakespeare text is an unstable and a contrived thing.

Often, of course, its judgements embody, if not the personal prejudices of the editor, then the cultural preferences of the time in which he or she was working. Growing awareness of this has led recent scholars to distrust the whole editorial enterprise and to repudiate the attempt to construct a 'perfect' text. Stanley Wells and Gary Taylor, the editors of the Oxford edition of *The Complete Works* (1988), point out that almost certainly the texts of Shakespeare's plays were altered in performance, and from one performance to another, so that there may never have been a single version. They note, too, that Shakespeare probably revised and rewrote some plays. They do not claim to print a definitive text of any play, but prefer what seems to them the 'more theatrical' version, and when there is a great difference between available versions, as with *King Lear*, they print two texts.

Shakespeare arrived in London at the very time that the Elizabethan period was poised to become the 'golden age' of English literature. Although Elizabeth reigned as queen from 1558 to 1603, the term 'Elizabethan' is used very loosely in a literary sense to refer to the period 1580 to 1625, when the great works of the age were produced. (Sometimes the later part of this period is distinguished as 'Jacobean', from the Latin form of James – James I of England and VI of Scotland reigned from 1603 to 1625.) The poet Edmund Spenser heralded this new age with his pastoral poem *The Shepheardes Calender* (1579) and in his essay *An Apologie for Poetrie* (written about 1580, although not published until 1595) his friend Sir Philip Sidney championed the imaginative power of the 'speaking picture of poesy', famously declaring that 'Nature never set forth the earth in so rich a tapestry as divers poets have done ... Her world is brazen, the poets only deliver a golden'.

Spenser and Sidney were part of that rejuvenating movement in European culture which since the nineteenth century has been known by the term *Renaissance*. Meaning literally *rebirth* it denotes a revival and redirection of artistic and intellectual endeavour which began in Italy in the fourteenth century in the poetry of **Petrarch**. It spread gradually northwards across Europe, and is first detectable in England in the early sixteenth century in the writings of the scholar and statesman Sir Thomas More and in the poetry of Sir Thomas Wyatt and Henry Howard, Earl of Surrey. Its keynote was a curiosity in thought which challenged old assumptions and traditions. To the innovative spirit of the Renaissance, the preceding ages appeared dully unoriginal and conformist.

That spirit was fuelled by the rediscovery of many Classical texts and the culture of Greece and Rome. This fostered a confidence in human reason and in human potential which, in every sphere, challenged old convictions. The discovery of America and its peoples (Columbus had sailed in 1492) demonstrated that the world was a larger and stranger place than had been thought. The cosmological speculation of Copernicus (later confirmed by Galileo) that the sun, not the earth was the centre of our planetary system challenged the centuries-old belief that the earth and human beings were at the centre of the cosmos. The pragmatic political philosophy of Machiavelli seemed to cut politics free from its traditional link with morality by permitting to statesmen any means which secured the desired end. And the religious movements we know collectively as the

Reformation broke with the Church of Rome and set the individual conscience, not ecclesiastical authority, at the centre of the religious life. Nothing, it seemed, was beyond questioning, nothing impossible.

Shakespeare's drama is innovative and challenging in exactly the way of the Renaissance. It questions the beliefs, assumptions and politics upon which Elizabethan society was founded. And although the plays always conclude in a restoration of order and stability, many critics are inclined to argue that their imaginative energy goes into subverting, rather than reinforcing, traditional values. They would point out that the famous speech on hierarchical order in *Troilus and Cressida* (I.3.86–124) or Katerina's speech on wifely submission to patriarchal authority in *The Taming of the Shrew* (V.2.146–60) appear to be rendered **ironic** by the action of the plays in which they occur. Convention, audience expectation and censorship all required the *status quo* to be endorsed by the plots' conclusions, but the dramas find ways to allow alternative sentiments to be expressed. Frequently, figures of authority are undercut by some comic or **parodic** figure: against the Duke in *Measure for Measure* is set Lucio; against Prospero in *The Tempest*, Caliban; against Henry IV, Falstaff. Despairing, critical, dissident, disillusioned, unbalanced, rebellious, mocking voices are repeatedly to be heard in the plays, rejecting, resenting, defying the established order. They belong always to marginal, socially unacceptable figures, 'licensed', as it were, by their situations to say what would be unacceptable from socially privileged or responsible citizens. The question is: are such characters given these views to discredit them, or were they the only ones through whom a voice could be given to radical and dissident ideas? Is Shakespeare a conservative or a revolutionary?

Renaissance culture was intensely nationalistic. With the break-up of the internationalism of the Middle Ages the evolving nation states which still mark the map of Europe began for the first time to acquire distinctive cultural identities. There was intense rivalry among them as they sought to achieve in their own vernacular languages a culture which could equal that of Greece and Rome. Spenser's great allegorical epic poem *The Faerie Queene*, which began to appear from 1590, celebrated Elizabeth and was intended to outdo the poetic achievements of France and Italy and to stand beside the works of Virgil and Homer. Shakespeare is equally preoccupied with national identity. His history plays tell an epic story which examines how modern England came into being through the conflicts of the fifteenth-century Wars of the Roses which brought the Tudors to the throne. He is fascinated, too, by the related subject of politics and the exercise of power. With the collapse of medieval feudalism and the authority of local barons, the royal court in the Renaissance came to assume a new status as the centre of power and patronage. It was here that the destiny of a country was shaped. Courts, and how to succeed in them, consequently fascinated the Renaissance; and they fascinated Shakespeare and his audience.

That is why we are usually at court in his plays, and in the company of courtiers. But the dramatic gaze is not merely admiring; through a variety of devices, a critical perspective is brought to bear. The court may be paralleled by a very different world, revealing uncomfortable similarities (for example, Henry's court and the Boar's Head tavern, ruled over by Falstaff in *Henry IV*). Its hypocrisy may be bitterly denounced (for example, in the diatribes of the mad Lear) and its self-seeking ambition represented disturbingly in the figure of a Machiavellian villain (such as Edmund in *Lear*) or a malcontent (such as Iago in *Othello*). Shakespeare is fond of displacing the court to another context, the better to examine its assumptions and pretensions and to offer alternatives to the courtly life (for example, in the pastoral setting of the forest of Arden in *As You Like It* or Prospero's island in *The Tempest*). Courtiers are frequently figures of fun whose unmanly sophistication ('neat and trimly dressed, / Fresh as a bridegroom ... perfumed like a milliner', says Hotspur of such a man in *Henry IV*, I.3.33–6) is contrasted with plain-speaking integrity: Oswald is set against Kent in *King Lear*.

(When thinking of these matters, we should remember that stage plays were subject to censorship, and any criticism had therefore to be muted or oblique: direct criticism of the monarch or contemporary English court would not be tolerated. This has something to do with why Shakespeare's plays are always set either in the past, or abroad.)

The nationalism of the English Renaissance was reinforced by Protestantism. Henry VIII had broken with Rome in the 1530s and in Shakespeare's time there was an independent Protestant state church. Because the Pope in Rome had excommunicated Queen Elizabeth as a heretic and relieved the English of their allegiance to the Crown, there was deep suspicion of Roman Catholics as potential traitors. This was enforced by the attempted invasion of the Spanish Armada in 1588. This was a

religiously inspired crusade to overthrow Elizabeth and restore England to
Roman Catholic allegiance. Roman Catholicism was hence easily identified
with hostility to England. Its association with disloyalty and treachery was
enforced by the Gunpowder Plot of 1605, a Roman Catholic attempt to
destroy the government of England.

Shakespeare's plays are remarkably free from direct religious senti-
ment, but their emphases are Protestant. Young women, for example, are
destined for marriage, not for nunneries (precisely what Isabella appears to
escape at the end of *Measure for Measure*); friars are dubious characters, full
of schemes and deceptions, if with benign intentions, as in *Much Ado About
Nothing* or *Romeo and Juliet*. (We should add, though, that Puritans,
extreme Protestants, are even less kindly treated: think of Malvolio in
Twelfth Night!) The central figures of the plays are frequently individuals
beset by temptation, by the lure of evil – Angelo in *Measure for Measure*,
Othello, Lear, Macbeth – and not only in tragedies: Falstaff is described as
'that old white-bearded Satan' (*1 Henry IV*, II.4.454). We follow their inner
struggles. Shakespeare's heroes have the preoccupation with self and the
introspective tendencies encouraged by Protestantism: his tragic heroes are
haunted by their consciences, seeking their true selves, agonising over what
course of action to take as they follow what can often be understood as a
kind of spiritual progress towards heaven or hell.

SHAKESPEARE'S THEATRE

The theatre for which the plays were written was one of the most
remarkable innovations of the Renaissance. There had been no theatres or
acting companies during the medieval period. Performed on carts and in
open spaces at Christian festivals, plays had been almost exclusively religious. Such professional actors as there were wandered the country putting
on a variety of entertainments in the yards of inns, on makeshift stages in
market squares, or anywhere else suitable. They did not perform full-length
plays, but mimes, juggling and comedy acts. Such actors were regarded by
officialdom and polite society as little better than vagabonds and layabouts.

Just before Shakespeare went to London all this began to change. A
number of young men who had been to the universities of Oxford and
Cambridge came to London in the 1580s and began to write plays which
made use of what they had learned about the Classical drama of ancient

Greece and Rome. Plays such as Lyly's *Alexander, Campaspe and Diogenes* (1584), Marlowe's *Tamburlaine the Great* (about 1587) and Thomas Kyd's *The Spanish Tragedy* (1588–9) were unlike anything that had been written in English before. They were full-length plays on secular subjects, taking their plots from history and legend, adopting many of the devices of Classical drama, and offering a range of characterisation and situation hitherto unattempted in English drama. With the exception of Lyly's prose dramas, they were in **blank verse** (unrhymed iambic pentameters) which the Earl of Surrey had introduced into English earlier in the sixteenth century. This was a freer and more expressive medium than the rhymed verse of medieval drama. It was the drama of these 'university wits' which Shakespeare challenged when he came to London. Greene was one of them, and we have heard how little he liked this Shakespeare setting himself up as a dramatist.

The most significant change of all, however, was that these dramatists wrote for the professional theatre. In 1576 James Burbage built the first permanent theatre in England, in Shoreditch, just beyond London's nor-thern boundary. It was called simply 'The Theatre'. Others soon followed. Thus, when Shakespeare came to London, there was a flourishing drama, theatres and companies of actors waiting for him, such as there had never been before in England. His company performed at James Burbage's Theatre until 1596, and used the Swan and Curtain until they moved into their own new theatre, the Globe, in 1599. (The Globe was burned down in 1613 when a cannon was fired during a performance of Shakespeare's *Henry VIII.*) We know that *Romeo and Juliet* was played at the Curtain, and, as a popular play, it would have been presented at the Globe as well.

With the completion in 1996 of Sam Wanamaker's project to con-struct in London a replica of The Globe, and with productions now running there, a version of Shakespeare's theatre can be experienced at first hand. It is very different to the usual modern experience of drama. The form of the Elizabethan theatre derived from the inn yards and animal baiting rings in which actors had been accustomed to perform in the past. They were circular wooden buildings with a paved courtyard in the middle open to the sky. A rectangular stage jutted out into the middle of this yard. Some of the audience stood in the yard (or 'pit') to watch the play. They were thus on three sides of the stage, close up to it and on a level with it. These 'groundlings' paid only a penny to get in, but for wealthier spectators there were seats in three covered tiers or galleries between the inner and outer walls of the building, extending round most of the auditorium and overlooking the pit and the stage. Such a theatre could hold about 3,000 spectators. The yards were just over 24 m. in diameter and the rectangular stage approximately 12 x 9 m. and 1.67 m high. Shakespeare aptly called such a theatre a 'wooden O' in the Prologue to *Henry V* (line 13).

The stage itself was partially covered by a roof or canopy which projected from the wall at the rear of the stage and was supported by two posts at the front. This protected the stage and performers from inclement weather, and to it were secured winches and other machinery for stage effects. On either side at the back of the stage was a door. These led into the dressing room (or 'tiring house') and it was by means of these doors that actors entered and left the stage. Between these doors was a small recess or alcove which was curtained off. Such a 'discovery place' served, for example, for Juliet's bedroom when in Act IV Scene 4 of *Romeo and Juliet* the Nurse went to the back of the stage and drew the curtain to find, or 'discover' in Elizabethan English, Juliet apparently dead on her bed. Above the discovery place was a balcony, used for the famous balcony scenes of *Romeo and Juliet* (II.2 and III.5), or for the battlements of Richard's castle when he is confronted by Bolingbroke in *Richard II* (III.3). Actors (all parts in the Elizabethan theatre were taken by boys or men) had access to the area beneath the stage; from here, in the 'cellarage', would have come the voice of the ghost of Hamlet's father (*Hamlet*, II.1.150–82).

On these stages there was very little in the way of scenery or props – there was nowhere to store them (there were no wings in this theatre) nor any way to set them up (no tabs across the stage), and, anyway, productions had to be transportable for performance at court or at noble houses. The stage was bare, which is why characters often tell us where they are: there was nothing on the stage to indicate location. It is also why location is so rarely topographical, and much more often symbolic. It suggests a dramatic mood or situation, rather than a place: Lear's barren heath reflects his destitute state, as the storm his emotional turmoil.

None of the plays printed in Shakespeare's lifetime marks Act or scene divisions. These have been introduced by later editors, but they should not mislead us into supposing that there was any break in Elizabethan performances such as might happen today while the curtains are closed and the set is changed. The staging of Elizabethan plays was continuous, with the many short 'scenes' of which Shakespeare's plays are often constructed following one after another in quick succession. We have to think of a more fluid, and much faster, production than we are generally used to: in the prologues to *Romeo and Juliet* (line 12) and *Henry VIII* (line 13) Shakespeare speaks of only two hours as the playing time.

We can see the kind of thing that happened from the stage directions in *Romeo and Juliet*. In I.4, Romeo and his friends decide to go to Capulet's party. At the end of the scene they 'march about the stage' while the serving-men come on to begin I.5. This represents their going into Capulet's house: there would have been no break in the actual performance. Again, in II.1, Mercutio and Benvolio are looking for Romeo. Failing to find him, they leave, and he 'comes forward' to begin II.2. His first line actually makes a rhyming verse **couplet** with Benvolio's last line of II.1. Clearly, although the scene of the action has changed (Mercutio and Benvolio are outside Capulet's garden; Romeo is inside it), there is no break in the play. Romeo comes straight on. A different kind of example occurs in III.5. This begins 'aloft', as the stage direction puts it, that is, on the balcony at the rear of the stage. When Romeo has left by climbing down to the stage, which here represents the garden (III.5.42), Juliet comes down by the stairs to the tiring house and enters the stage through one of the rear doors to meet her mother in the house (III.5.64–5). In this scene, then, the stage has represented two different places (the garden and the interior of the house) but the acting goes on regardless.

It is because of this continuous staging and the lack of scenery that characters in Shakespeare's plays often tell the audience what locality the stage represents at different moments. Romeo's last words in II.2, for example, set the scene for II.3. Similarly, Romeo's words at II.2.107–8 create the scene in the imagination of the audience. On the other hand, we often cannot tell where a scene is set. There is no evidence in the text, for example, for the locality of I.2 or II.4 of *Romeo and Juliet*. Modern editors often supply a locale for such scenes, but it can be safely assumed that if Shakespeare's characters do not say where they are, then their location does not matter much. The lack of a curtain across the stage in the Elizabethan theatre explains why scenes often end with rhyming lines. These show the audience that the scene has ended, and prepare them for a new scene (for example, the final two lines of V. 1 in *Romeo and Juliet*). And because actors were in full view from the moment they set foot on the stage, entrances and exits had to be written in as part of the play. Characters speak as they enter or leave the stage because otherwise there would have been a silence while, in full view, they took up their positions (for example, in *Romeo and Juliet*, I.3.1–5; I.4.113–4; I.5.144). For the same reason, dead bodies had always to be removed by the actors in the course of the play: they cannot get up and walk off (so Mercutio goes off-stage to die and Tybalt's body is carried off, III. 1.108, 196).

In 1608 Shakespeare's company, the King's Men, acquired the Blackfriars Theatre, a smaller, rectangular indoor theatre, holding about 700 people, with seats for all the members of the audience, facilities for elaborate stage effects and, because it was enclosed, artificial lighting. It has been suggested that the plays written for this 'private' theatre differed from those written for the Globe, since, as it cost more to go to a private theatre, the audience came from a higher social stratum and demanded the more elaborate and courtly entertainment which Shakespeare's romances provide. However, the King's Men continued to play in the Globe in the summer, using Blackfriars in the winter, and it is not certain that Shakespeare's last plays were written specifically for the Blackfriars Theatre, or first performed there.

READING SHAKESPEARE

Shakespeare's plays were written for this stage, but there is also a sense in which they were written *by* this stage. The material and physical circumstances of their production in such theatres had a profound effect upon the nature of Elizabethan plays. Unless we bear this in mind, we are likely to find them very strange, for we will read with expectations shaped by our own familiarity with modern fiction and modern drama. This is, by and large, realistic; it seeks to persuade us that what we are reading or watching is really happening. This is quite foreign to Shakespeare. If we try to read him like this, we shall find ourselves irritated by the improbabilities of his plot, confused by his chronology, puzzled by locations, frustrated by unanswered questions and dissatisfied by the motivation of the action. The absurd ease with which disguised persons pass through Shakespeare's plays is a case in point: why does no-one recognise people they know so well? There is a great deal of psychological accuracy in Shakespeare's plays, but we are far from any attempt at realism.

The reason is that in Shakespeare's theatre it was impossible to pretend that the audience was not watching a contrived performance. In a modern theatre, the audience is encouraged to forget itself as it becomes absorbed by the action on stage. The worlds of the spectators and of the actors are sharply distinguished by the lighting: in the dark auditorium the audience is passive, silent, anonymous, receptive and attentive; on the lighted stage the actors are active, vocal, demonstrative and dramatic. (The distinction is, of course, still more marked in the cinema.) There is no communication between the two worlds: for the audience to speak would be interruptive; for the actors to address the audience would be to break the illusion of the play. In the Elizabethan theatre, this distinction did not exist, and for two reasons: first, performances took place in the open air and in daylight which illuminated everyone equally; secondly, the spectators were all around the stage (and wealthier spectators actually on it), and were dressed no differently to the actors, who wore contemporary dress. In such a theatre, spectators would be as aware of each other as of the actors; they could not lose their identity in a corporate group, nor could they ever forget that they were spectators at a performance. There was no chance that they could believe 'this is really happening'.

This, then, was communal theatre, not only in the sense that it was going on in the middle of a crowd but in the sense that the crowd joined in. Elizabethan audiences had none of our deference: they did not keep quiet, or arrive on time, or remain for the whole performance. They joined in, interrupted, even getting on the stage. And plays were preceded and followed by jigs and clowning. It was all much more like our experience of a pantomime, and at a pantomime we are fully aware, and are meant to be aware, that we are watching games being played with reality. The conventions of pantomime revel in their own artificiality: the Dame's monstrous false breasts signal that 'she' is a man.

Something very similar is the case with Elizabethan theatre: it utilised its very theatricality. Instead of trying to persuade spectators that they are not in a theatre watching a performance, Elizabethan plays acknowledge the presence of the audience. It is addressed not only by prologues, epilogues and choruses, but in **soliloquies**. There is no realistic reason why characters should suddenly explain themselves to empty rooms, but, of course, it is not an empty room. The actor is surrounded by people. Soliloquies are not addressed to the world of the play: they are for the audience's benefit. And that audience's complicity is assumed: when a character like Prospero declares himself to be invisible, it is accepted that he is. Disguises are taken to be impenetrable, however improbable, and we are to accept impossibly contrived situations, such as barely hidden characters remaining undetected (indeed, on the Elizabethan stage there was nowhere at all they could hide!).

These, then, are plays which are aware of themselves as dramas; in critical terminology, they are self-reflexive, commenting upon themselves as dramatic pieces and prompting the audience to think about the theatrical experience. They do this not only through their direct address to the audience but through their fondness for the play-within-a-play (which reminds the audience that the encompassing play is also a play) and their constant use of images from, and allusions to, the theatre. They are fascinated by role playing, by acting, appearance and reality. Things are rarely what they seem, either in comedy (for example, in *A Midsummer Night's Dream*) or tragedy (*Romeo and Juliet*). This offers one way to think about those disguises: they are thematic rather than realistic. Kent's disguise in *Lear* reveals his true, loyal self, while Edmund, who is not disguised, hides his true self. In *As You Like It*, Rosalind is more truly herself disguised as a man than when dressed as a woman.

The effect of all this is to confuse the distinction we would make between 'real life' and 'acting'. The case of Rosalind, for example, raises searching questions about gender roles, about how far it is 'natural' to be womanly or manly: how does the stage, on which a man can play a woman playing a man (and have a man fall in love with him/her!), differ from life, in which we assume the roles we think appropriate to masculine and feminine behaviour? The same is true of political roles: when a Richard II or Lear is so aware of the regal part he is performing, of the trappings and rituals of kingship, their plays raise the uncomfortable possibility that the answer to the question, what constitutes a successful king, is simply: a good actor. Indeed, human life generally is repeatedly rendered through the imagery of the stage, from Macbeth's 'Life's but a walking shadow, a poor player / That struts and frets his hour upon the stage / And then is heard no more …' (V.5.23–5) to Prospero's paralleling of human life to a performance which, like the globe (both world and theatre) will end (IV.I.146–58). When life is a fiction, like this play, or this play is a fiction like life, what is the difference? 'All the world's a stage …' (*As You Like It*, II.7.139).

PART SIX

CRITICAL HISTORY

TRADITIONAL CRITICISM

Eighteenth-century criticism of Shakespeare was concerned chiefly with the structure of his plays and the extent to which this did, or did not, conform to the model of Classical drama, though the early eighteenth-century poet Alexander Pope, who edited Shakespeare's works, pointedly remarked that 'To judge … of Shakespeare by Aristotle's rules, is like trying a man by the Laws of one Country, who acted under those of another'. It was in reaction to the judgemental, and often censorious, tenor of much eighteenth-century criticism that the poets and critics of the Romantic period came to champion Shakespeare's genius, imagination and passion as far more important than matters of plot and structure. These qualities were discerned in Shakespeare's poetry, and in the authenticity this gave to the feelings of his characters. For the Romantic critic and poet Samuel Taylor Coleridge they were especially in evidence in *Romeo and Juliet*. In lectures on the play he commended the variety of its language, the individuality of its characters and the power of its depiction of passionate feeling.

This line in criticism culminated in A. C. Bradley's immensely influential *Shakespearean Tragedy* (1904), which treated Shakespeare's characters not as parts of a dramatic design but as living persons, each with a personal history and a fully developed psychology which could be analysed. He interpreted the action of the tragedies (though his book did not include a chapter on *Romeo and Juliet*) in terms of the personality and choices of their tragic heroes. This approach was famously mocked in an essay entitled 'How many children had Lady Macbeth?' by L. C. Knights (1933).

DECONSTRUCTION AND HISTORICISM

Following Knights, recent criticism has lost interest in characterisation. Contemporary studies are concerned much more, first, with the complexity of texts and the way that their apparent meanings are contradicted and problematised. This deconstructive approach seeks to bring out the tensions within texts and to challenge the claim that texts have a single meaning, which is what their authors intended them to mean. It is exemplified in the essays collected in John Drakakis's aptly entitled *Alternative Shakespeares* (1985).

Secondly, critics have been interested in the ways texts are shaped not by their author's intentions but by the societies and cultures which produced them, and in the extent to which they either reinforce, or work against, the political and social power systems of their time. New historicists tend to argue that the *status quo* is confirmed by textual representations of power while cultural materialists (often of a Marxist persuasion) such as Jonathan Dollimore look out for passages of resistance to institutional authority. Both are interested in how far the subversive tendencies of texts are contained. Such an approach would seek to establish how far the re-establishment of traditional order at the end of *Romeo and Juliet* closes down the challenge to that order posed by the actions of the lovers.

The reading offered in the Critical Approaches in this Note has explored the ways in which the love of Romeo and Juliet is vindicated. However, approaches of a deconstructive and historicist caste might challenge that, on the grounds of what the play does not mention and what the audience might be expected to have brought to it. An uncomfortable silence is maintained about one conspicuous feature of the plot, namely, the suicide of Romeo and Juliet. The silence is uncomfortable because everyone in the Elizabethan audience would have known that suicide is a mortal sin, that there could be no burial in consecrated ground for suicides and that they had lost all hope of salvation. The play is silent on this because, of course, to introduce the notion that Romeo and Juliet are damned would run entirely against its celebration of their love. In fact, however, its silence only alerts us to the omission, for the fact would have been so glaringly obvious as to be inescapable. It is all but inconceivable that, at the end of the play, neither the Friar nor the Prince should mention it. This tension between the play's text and its cultural context problematises it in other ways: Romeo and Juliet are passionate lovers, utterly immoderate in their obsession with each other, quite incapable of compromise (as the Friar reminds us). It is this, as much as any external force, which brings them to their deaths; it is this which presents suicide to them as the only possible course. The Christian tradition and the Classical tradition, taken up by the Elizabethan world, valued restraint, moderation and reasonableness very highly. It regarded surrender to one's passion as a surrender of the capacity to make rational choices; it was to be driven by wilful desire, and so to act sinfully. Although this theme is much less pronounced in Shakespeare's play than in his sources (see Shakespeare's Use of Sources), it nevertheless cannot be written out of the story so completely as the text would wish. There is justice in their deaths since Romeo and Juliet bring their fate upon themselves through their worship of each other to the exclusion of all other moral obligations. The play retains the profile of an admonitory tale.

THE FEMINIST APPROACH

A third strand in contemporary criticism is that of feminism. This is interested in the depiction of women, in the predominance of the male voice and gaze, in the structuring of texts by patriarchal assumptions, and in the ways in which notions of woman's inferior place are (or are not) reproduced. This approach would be interested in Capulet's assumption of the right to dispose of his daughter to another man, in Juliet's initial submission to her father's patriarchal authority (mirrored in the state by the authority exercised over his subjects by the Prince) and in her later repudiation of it. It can suggest (as does Cedric Watts in his study of the play) that the championing of the lovers in *Romeo and Juliet* issues a challenge to traditional notions of familial duty, gender relations and the character and status of women, but it could also argue that the structure of the play insists that Juliet's insubordination is punished. Everyone at the end may be chastened, but Juliet does not get away with her rebellion. Feminist critics would also ask how far the Nurse is a liberated figure, refreshingly free from inhibitions about sex, and how far trapped in a marginal role as a woman whose usefulness really ceased when she could no longer breastfeed Juliet. However, though the Nurse might seem trapped in a world of smutty jokes and garrulity, Juliet exhibits a determination, resolution and circumspection rather beyond Romeo. It is she, rather than he, who is in charge. On the other hand, it is her love for a man (and not her friendship with the Nurse) which gives her this strength.

These various contemporary approaches characteristically think of themselves as radical and committed to a left-of-centre politics; they believe that traditional readings of Shakespeare have been contrived (or 'fabricated', they are fond of saying) to support conservative thinking, traditionalism and the politics of the right. They believe that Shakespeare has been appropriated to serve the *status quo* (Prince Charles's publicly stated admiration for him might be cited). As Kiernan Ryan puts it in his lucid summary of these approaches in the opening chapter of his *Shakespeare*, 'The problem is that so far the battle for the Bard has invariably been won by forces intent on fabricating from his life and art a powerful apology for leaving the world the way it is'. The belligerent imagery here (criticism becomes a 'battle') suggests self-interest in traditional criticism, if not a deliberate plot; it is equated with 'forces intent' on resisting political change. One might remark that criticism such as Ryan's is still less impartial, his political commitment still more overt; but to this the reply would be that all criticism is political.

PART SEVEN

BROADER PERSPECTIVES

FURTHER READING

OTHER POPULAR EDITIONS OF ROMEO AND JULIET

Romeo and Juliet, Penguin Popular Classics, 1994

>Much the cheapest edition available. It has a chronological list of Shakespeare's plays, a brief introduction, notes and glossary, and a most interesting reconstruction of an Elizabethan performance on the basis of the stage directions in both Q1 and Q2

J.A. Bryant, Jr, ed., *Romeo and Juliet*, The Signet Classic Shakespeare, New English Library, 1964

>A useful introduction and glossaries on the same page as the text, which saves the reader having to refer to the back of the book. There is no commentary on the text, but there are helpful excerpts from critical studies of the play and a discussion of the text and sources

Brian Gibbons, ed., *Romeo and Juliet*, The Arden Shakespeare, Routledge, 1980

>An up-to-date scholarly edition, with a long introduction discussing the text, date, sources and literary qualities of the play, and very full notes on each page which explain vocabulary, allusions and points of detail

G. Blakemore, ed., *Romeo and Juliet*, New Cambridge Shakespeare, Cambridge University Press, 1984

>Another scholarly edition which may be consulted on all textual and critical matters

GENERAL WORKS

Jonathan Dollimore, *Radical Tragedy: Religion, Ideology and Power in the drama of Shakespeare and his Contemporaries*, 2nd edn, Harvester, 1989

>A cultural materialist account of Elizabethan drama as critically subversive

John Drakakis, ed., *Alternative Shakespeares*, New Accents, Methuen, 1985

>A seminal collection of contemporary approaches to Shakespeare

– *Shakespearean Tragedy*, Longman Critical Readers 1992
> A collection of contemporary theoretical approaches, with an essay on *Romeo and Juliet* by Julia Kristeva

Juliet Dusinberre, *Shakespeare and the Nature of Women*, Macmillan, 1975
> An excellent introduction to the subject

Terry Eagleton, *William Shakespeare*, Blackwell, 1986
> A lively and accessible account of Shakespeare in the light of deconstruction, feminism and Marxism

Andrew Gurr, *The Shakespearean Stage, 1574–1642*, 3rd edn, Cambridge University Press, 1992
> The standard work on the subject

Lisa Jardine, *Still Harping on Daughters: women and drama in the age of Shakespeare*, Harvester, 1983
> A feminist account of notions about, and the depiction of, women in the Elizabethan age and in Shakespeare with many observations relevant to *Romeo and Juliet*

Kiernan Ryan, *Shakespeare*, 2nd edn, Harvester, 1995
> Surveys contemporary approaches to Shakespeare and has a section challenging traditional readings of *Romeo and Juliet*

S. Schoenbaum, *William Shakespeare: a Compact Documentary Life*, Clarendon Press, 1977
> The most authoritative biography

CRITICAL STUDIES OF ROMEO AND JULIET

Samuel Taylor Coleridge, *Shakespearean Criticism*, ed.T. M. Raysor, 2 vols, Dent, 1960
> Includes a lecture and several passages on the play

Nicholas Brooke, *Shakespeare's Early Tragedies*, Methuen, 1968
> Discusses the patterning of the play in language and structure

J.R. Brown, and B. Harris, eds., *Early Shakespeare*, Stratford-upon-Avon Studies III, Arnold, 1961
> Includes an essay by John Lawlor on *Romeo and Juliet* as a medieval tragedy

G. Bullough, ed., *Narrative and Dramatic Sources of Shakespeare*, 7 vols, Routledge, 1957–73
> Vol I reprints Arthur Brooke's poem *The Tragicall Historye of Romeus and Juliet*

Douglas Cole, ed., *Twentieth-century Interpretations of Romeo and Juliet*, Prentice-Hall, 1970
> A collection of appreciative essays

Franklin Dickey, *Not Wisely But Too Well: Shakespeare's Tragedies of Love*, Huntingdon Library, San Marino CA 1957
> Ideas of love in the play seen as a Christian tragedy

H. Granville Barker, *Prefaces to Shakespeare*, 2 vols, Batsford, 1958
> Especially on how the play might best be presented in the theatre

A.C. Hamilton, *The Early Shakespeare*, Huntington Library, 1967
> The play in relation to the comedies

G.B. Harrison, *Shakespeare's Tragedies*, Routledge, 1951
> A very useful introductory essay

L. Lerner, ed., *Shakespeare's Tragedies: An Anthology of Modern Criticism*, Penguin, 1963
> Includes extracts from M.M. Mahood, *Shakespeare's Wordplay*, London, 1957, an excellent discussion of the quibbling and punning in the play, and C. Williams, *The English Poetic Mind*, London, 1932

H.A. Mason, *Shakespeare's Tragedies of Love*, Chatto and Windus, 1970
> Discusses particularly the relationship between Shakespeare's treatment of love and the tragedy

O.H. Moore, *The Legend of Romeo and Juliet*, Ohio State University Press, 1950
> A full account of the development of the Romeo and Juliet story

Leah Scragg, *Shakespeare's Mouldy Tales*, Longman, 1992
> Accessible discussion of Shakespeare's manipulation of his sources, with a section on *Romeo and Juliet*

T.J.B. Spencer, ed., *Elizabethan Love Stories*, Penguin, 1968
> Reprints William Painter's version of the Romeo and Juliet story

E.E. Stoll, *Shakespeare's Young Lovers*, Oxford University Press, 1937
> A fine essay on the characters of Romeo and Juliet and the nature of their love

J. Vyvyan, *Shakespeare and the Rose of Love*, Chatto & Windus, 1968
> Ideas of love in the play

Cedric Watts, *Romeo and Juliet*, Harvester New Critical Introductions, Harvester, 1991
> An excellent account of the play, paying particular attention to its sexual politics and to the interplay of lyricism and bawdy in its dramatisation of love

World events	Shakespeare's life	Literature and the arts
		1374 Death of Petrarch, most popular poet of the Italian Renaissance
		1476 Masuccio Salernitano writes original tale of Romeo and Juliet
		1487 Matteomaria Boiardo, *Orlando Innamorato*, the love story of Orlando and Angelica
1492 Columbus sails to America		
		1513 Niccolò Machiavelli, *The Prince*
		1528 Castiglione's *Book of the Courtier*
		1532 Ludovico Ariosto, *Orlando Furioso* continues Boiardo's love story
1534 Henry VIII breaks with Rome and declares himself head of the Church of England		
1556 Archbishop Cranmer burnt at the stake		
1558 Elizabeth I accedes to throne		
		1562 Arthur Brooke, *The Tragicall Historye of Romeus and Juliet*. Birth of Lope de Vega, Spanish dramatist
	1564 (26 April) William Shakespeare baptised, Stratford-upon-Avon	
		1567 William Painter, 'The goodly History of the true and constant love between Rhomeo and Julietta'
1568 Mary Queen of Scots taken prisoner by Elizabeth I		
1570 Elizabeth I excommunicated by Pope Pius V		
1571 The Battle of Lepanto		
		1576 James Burbage builds the first theatre in England, at Shoreditch
1577 Francis Drake sets out on round the world voyage		
		1579 Edmund Spenser, *The Shepheardes Calender*
		1580 (c.) Sir Philip Sidney, *An Apologie for Poetrie*
1582 Outbreak of the Plague in London	**1582** He marries Anne Hathaway	
	1583 His daughter, Susanna, born	
		1584 John Lyly's *Alexander, Campaspe and Diogenes*
1584 Raleigh's sailors land in Virginia	**1585** His twins, Hamnet and Judith, born	
1587 Execution of Mary Queen of Scots after implication in plot to murder Elizabeth I		
		1587 Christopher Marlowe, *Tamburlaine the Great*
	late 1580s - early 90s He probably writes *Henry VI (Parts I, II, III)* and *Richard III*	

World events	Shakespeare's life	Literature and the arts
		1588-9 Thomas Kyd, *The Spanish Tragedy*
1588 The Spanish Armada defeated		
1589 Accession of Henri IV to French throne		
		1590 Edmund Spenser, *The Faerie Queene (Books I-III)*
		1591 Sir John Harington translates *Orlando Furioso* into English
1592 Plague in London closes theatres	**1592** Shakespeare recorded as being a London actor and an 'upstart crow'	
	1592-4 He writes *Comedy of Errors*	
	1594 onwards, He writes exclusively for the Lord Chamberlain's Men	
	1594 *The Comedy of Errors* first acted	
	1595 (c.) His *Two Gentlemen of Verona, The Taming of the Shrew* and *Love's Labour's Lost* are thought to have been written before this year. He writes *Romeo and Juliet*	
1596 Drake perishes on expedition to West Indies		
		1598-9 Globe Theatre built at Southwark
	1600 *A Midsummer Night's Dream, Much Ado about Nothing* and *The Merchant of Venice* printed; *Twelfth Night* probably written	
	1600-1 Shakespeare's *Hamlet*	
	1602 His *Troilus and Cressida* probably written	
1603 Death of Queen Elizabeth I	**1603** onwards, his company enjoys patronage of James I as the King's Men	
	1604 His *Othello* performed	
1605 Discovery of Guy Fawkes's plot to blow up the Houses of Parliament	**1605** First version of his *King Lear*	**1605** Cervantes, *Don Quijote de la Mancha*
	1606 He writes *Macbeth*	
	1606-7 He probably writes *Antony and Cleopatra*	
	1608 The King's Men acquire Blackfriars Theatre for winter performances	
1609 Galileo constructs first astronomical telescope		
1610 Henri IV of France assassinated William Harvey discovers circulation of blood Galileo observes Saturn for the first time		
	1611 Shakespeare's *Cymbeline, The Winter's Tale* and *The Tempest* performed	
1612 Last burning of heretics in England		
	1613 Globe Theatre burns down	
	1616 Death of William Shakespeare	
1618 Raleigh executed for treason Thirty Years War begins in England		
		1622 Birth of French dramatist Molière

blank verse unrhymed lines of five stresses (iambic pentameter)

conceit extended image

couplet a pair of rhymed lines

crux textual passage which puzzles commentators

Elizabethan wit clever inventiveness, ingenious dexterity with words, all containing the idea of surprise and unexpectedness

hyperbole emphasis by exaggeration

iambic pentameter a line of five stresses

irony saying one thing while meaning another; **tragic/dramatic irony** occurs when the audience knows more than the play's characters and can foresee the outcome

metaphor figure of speech in which something is spoken of as *being* that which it resembles

multivocal speaking with more than one voice

multivalent having more than one meaning

oxymoron combination of words of opposite meanings

parody an imitation of a style or work of literature designed to ridicule the original

Petrarch fourteenth-century Italian poet who gave his name to **Petrarchan (or courtly) love**, which idealised womanhood, and the Petrarchan sonnet (see sonnet)

quarto book made up of paper sheets folded to make four leaves

quatrain a stanza of four lines

self-reflexive plays that comment upon themselves as dramatic pieces

soliloquy a speech delivered by a character when alone, enabling him or her to reveal innermost thoughts and motivations

sonnet lyric poem consisting of fourteen rhyming lines of iambic pentameter; **Elizabethan/Shakespearian sonnet**, usually rhyming abab cdcd efef gg; **Petrarchan sonnet**, abba abba cdd cdd or cde cde

verisimilitude likeness to reality

Professor N.H. Keeble is currently Head of the Department of English Studies at the University of Stirling, where he has taught for twenty years. During this time he has regularly run courses on Shakespeare. His research lies in the early modern period and he has published widely on English literature of the sixteenth and seventeenth centuries.